MEN MADE NEW

an exposition of Romans 5—8 by John R. W. Stott

John Stott.

Inter-Varsity Press
Downers Grove, Illinois 60515

Inter-Varsity Press is the
book publishing division of the
Inter-Varsity Christian Fellowship.

Library of Congress Catalog card number: 66-24396

Printed in the United States of America

CONTENTS

COMMENTARIES

Works referred to in the text are:

F. F. BRUCE   *The Epistle of Paul to the Romans*, An Introduction and Commentary, by F. F. Bruce (Tyndale Press, 1963)

E. F. KEVAN   *The Saving Work of the Holy Spirit* (Keswick Bible Readings 1953 on Rom. 7:14—8:27) by E. F. Kevan (Pickering and Inglis)

H. P. LIDDON   *Explanatory Analysis of St Paul's Epistle to the Romans* by H. P. Liddon (Longmans Green, 1893)

C. J. VAUGHAN   *St Paul's Epistle to the Romans* by C. J. Vaughan (Macmillan, 1859)

ACKNOWLEDGMENT

The author desires to acknowledge his gratitude to the Keswick Council for inviting him to give the Bible Readings on Romans 5—8 at the Keswick Convention in July 1965, and in particular to Canon A. T. Houghton, Chairman of the Council, for his personal encouragement. It was a great inspiration to be allowed to expound the Word of God to about 5,000 people for a whole hour on four successive mornings in the big tent. The text of the Bible Readings given then, which appeared in *The Life of Faith* in the weeks following the Convention, has here been somewhat amplified for publication.

INTRODUCTION

The Epistle to the Romans is the fullest and most coherent manifesto of the Christian gospel in the New Testament. In it the apostle Paul unfolds 'the whole counsel of God'—man's sin and lostness, Christ's death to save him, faith in Christ as the sole condition of his acceptance, the work of the Holy Spirit for his growth in holiness, the place of Israel in the purpose of God, and the ethical implications of the gospel. There is a grandeur, a comprehensiveness, a logic about his exposition which has commanded the admiration and compelled the study of all succeeding generations.

It is dangerous to isolate four chapters from the Epistle's sixteen, but the exigencies of four one-hour Bible Readings at a one-week convention made it necessary, and chapters 5–8 do form a compact unity.

They are without doubt among the greatest and most glorious chapters of the whole New Testament. They portray our Christian privilege, the privileges of those whom God has 'made new', those whom He has 'justified', that is, declared righteous and accepted in Christ. The earlier chapters of the Epistle are devoted to the need and the way of justification. They are concerned to make it plain that all men are sinners under the just judgment of God, and can be justified solely through the redemption which is in Christ Jesus—by grace alone, through faith alone. Now, at this point, having set forth the need and explained the way of justification, Paul goes on to describe its fruits, the results of justification in a life of sonship and obedience on earth and a glorious hereafter in heaven.

This is very important, because there are too many of us who think and behave as if the gospel were good news of justification only, and not good news also of holiness and of heaven. We speak as if, having come to God through Jesus Christ, we had arrived, full stop, and that was the finish. We talk as if we had come to a dead end; as if there were no further road to travel. But this is not so. The very first verse of this chapter begins with the words, 'Therefore, since we are justified by faith . . .'. That is to say: now that we are justified, these are the consequences, these are the fruits, of our justification. Having been brought into acceptance with God through trust in Jesus Christ, this is what follows.

These four chapters, then, depict the great privileges of justified believers, of *Men Made New*, the rich inheritance (both now and in eternity) which is ours if we are Christ's. What are these privileges? Each chapter concentrates on one of them: first *peace with God* (chapter 5), next *union with Christ* (chapter 6), then *freedom from the law* (chapter 7), and finally *life in the Spirit* (chapter 8). We shall examine each in turn.

CHAPTER ONE

PEACE WITH GOD

Romans 5:1–19

Romans 5 divides clearly into two distinct paragraphs. The first eleven verses portray the fruits or results of our justification, while verses 12–19 show us the Mediator of our justification, the One through whom justification has come to us—namely Jesus Christ, the second Adam.

I. THE FRUITS OF OUR JUSTIFICATION
(5:1–11)

Therefore, since we are justified by faith, we have peace with God through our Lord Jesus Christ. Through him we have obtained access to this grace in which we stand, and we rejoice in our hope of sharing the glory of God. More than that, we rejoice in our sufferings, knowing that suffering produces endurance, and endurance produces character, and character produces hope, and hope does not disappoint us, because God's love has been poured into our hearts through the Holy Spirit which has been given to us.

While we were yet helpless, at the right time Christ died for the ungodly. Why, one will hardly die for a righteous man—though perhaps for a good man one will dare even to die. But God shows his love for us in that while we were yet sinners Christ died for us. Since, therefore, we are now justified by his blood, much more shall we be saved by him from the wrath of God. For if while we were enemies we were reconciled to God by the death of his Son, much more, now that we are reconciled, shall we be saved by his life. Not only so, but we also rejoice in God through our Lord Jesus Christ, through whom we have now received our reconciliation.[1]

a. The fruits described (verses 1, 2)

Here we have a summary of the results of justification in three sentences. First, 'we have peace with God through our Lord Jesus Christ' (verse 1). Secondly (verse 2a), we have 'obtained access (through the same Christ and through the same faith) to this grace in which we stand'. Thirdly (verse 2b), 'we rejoice in our hope of sharing the glory of God.' Here are the fruits of our justification: Peace, grace and glory. Peace with God (which we have), grace (in which we stand), and glory (for which we hope).

On a closer examination these appear to relate to the three tenses or phases of our salvation. 'Peace with God' speaks of the *immediate* effect of justification. We were 'enemies' of God (verse 10), but now the old enmity has been put away by God's forgiveness and we are at peace with Him. The immediate effect of justification, then, is that enmity has given way to peace.

Secondly, 'this grace in which we stand' speaks of the *continuing* effect of justification. It is a state of grace to which we have obtained access and in which we continue to stand. This is how the New English Bible puts it: 'We have been allowed to enter the sphere of God's grace.' And, of course, having entered it we continue in it. We stand in it today.

[1] The biblical text used and all quotations are from the Revised Standard Version (1946–52), unless otherwise stated.

Thirdly, 'the glory of God' for which we hope speaks of the *ultimate* effect of justification. 'The glory of God' here means heaven, because in heaven God Himself will be fully revealed ('glory' in biblical language is the manifestation of God). We are going to see God's glory in heaven, and even share in it (since then we shall be like Christ, 1 Jn. 3:2). 'Hope' is our sure and certain confidence or expectation. This is 'the hope of glory', for which we give thanks in the General Thanksgiving. Indeed, so sure is this hope (what J. B. Phillips calls this 'happy certainty') that we can rejoice in it now already. 'We rejoice in our hope (that is, in our certain confidence) of . . . the glory of God.'

These three phrases paint a balanced picture of the Christian life in relation to God. There is nothing here about our relation to our neighbour, but as far as our relation to God is concerned they constitute a beautiful summary of the Christian life: Peace, grace, and glory. In the word 'peace' we look back to the enmity which is now over. In the word 'grace' we look up to our reconciled Father in whose favour we now continue to stand. In the word 'glory' we look on to our final destiny, seeing and reflecting the glory of God, which is the object of our hope or expectation.

b. *Suffering, the pathway to glory* (verses 3, 4)

This does not mean to say, of course, that after justification the narrow way is carpeted all along with moss and primroses. No; brambles grow on it, too, and brambles with sharp thorns. 'More than that,' says Paul in verse 3, 'we rejoice in our sufferings.' Peace, grace, glory—yes, but suffering as well.

Now these sufferings, strictly speaking, are not sickness or pain, sorrow or bereavement, but tribulation (*thlipsis*), the pressure of a godless and hostile world.

Yet such suffering is always the pathway to glory.
The risen Lord Himself said so. He declared that,
according to the Old Testament, the Christ must
suffer and so enter into His glory (Lk. 24:26). And
what is true of Christ is true of the Christian as well,
since the servant is not greater than his Lord. Paul
himself says so later, in Romans 8:17: 'provided we
suffer with him (Christ) in order that we may also be
glorified with him.'

Note carefully the relation between our present sufferings and our future glory. It is not just that the one
is the way to the other. Still less is it that we grin and
bear the one in anticipation of the other. No. According to the text the relation between the two is the
element of rejoicing: we rejoice in both. If we 'rejoice'
in our hope of glory (verse 2), we 'rejoice' in our sufferings as well (verse 3). And the verb is a strong one
(*kauchōmetha*). It indicates, as the NEB renders it, that
we 'exult' in them. Present suffering and future glory
are both objects of a Christian's exultation. How is
this? How can we possibly rejoice in our sufferings?
How can we find joy in what causes us pain? Verses
3-5 explain the paradox.

It is not that we rejoice in the sufferings themselves,
so much as in their beneficial results. We are not
masochists who enjoy being hurt. We are not even
Stoics who grit their teeth and endure. We are Christians, who see in our sufferings the outworking of a
gracious, divine purpose. We rejoice because of what
suffering 'produces'. That is the word the RSV chooses:
'Suffering produces endurance, and endurance produces character.' It is because of what suffering *produces* (*katergazetai*) that we rejoice in it. Well, then,
what are the outworkings of tribulation? The process
is given us in three stages.

Stage 1: suffering produces endurance. That is, the

very endurance we need in suffering is produced by it, much as antibodies are produced in the human body by infection. We could not learn endurance without suffering, because without suffering there would be nothing to endure. So suffering produces endurance.

Stage 2: endurance produces character (AV 'experience'). 'Character' (*dokimē*) is the quality of someone who, or something which, has been put to the test and come through it. It is the quality which David's armour lacked, when he said he could not wear it because he had not 'proved' it; he had not put it to the test. Can we not usually recognize the mature character of a Christian who has gone through suffering and come out triumphant? 'Suffering produces endurance, and endurance produces character.'

Stage 3: character produces hope. That is, confidence of the final glory. The maturity of character born of past endurance of suffering brings with it a hope of future glory. What the apostle means is surely this, that our developing, ripening Christian character is evidence that God is at work upon us and within us. The fact that God is thus at work in our lives gives us confidence that He is not going to give up the job uncompleted. If He is working in us now to transform our character, He is surely going to bring us safely to glory in the end. The apostle is back, you see, to the indissoluble link between suffering and glory. The reason why, if we rejoice in hope of the glory of God, we rejoice in our sufferings also, is that our sufferings produce the hope of this glory. If the hope of glory is produced by sufferings, then we rejoice in the sufferings as well as the glory. We rejoice not only in the end (glory), but in the means to the end (suffering). We rejoice in them both.

c. Assurance grounded in the love of God (verse 5)

Someone may well ask—and Paul anticipates the question—'How can you know this hope of glory has any substance to it? How can you know that it is not just wishful thinking? It is all very well to say you are going to heaven—to glory—but how do you know?' Paul says, first of all, 'Hope does not disappoint us.' That is, hope *will* not disappoint us. The NEB reads: 'Such a hope (of glory) is no mockery.' It is a true hope. 'Yes, Paul,' the questioner goes on, 'that is what you *say*, but how do you *know*? How can you be so sure that your Christian hope will never disappoint you?' Paul's answer is in the rest of verse 5, where he says we know that hope will never disappoint us '*because* God's love has been poured out in our hearts through the Holy Spirit who was given to us' (literally). The solid foundation on which our hope of glory rests is the love of God. It is because God has set His love upon us that we know, beyond any question or doubt, that He is going to bring us to glory. We believe that we are going to persevere to the end, and we have good grounds for our confidence. It is partly because of the character God is forming in us through suffering that we can be confident ('suffering—endurance—character—hope'). If He is sanctifying us now, He will surely glorify us then. But it is chiefly because of 'the love that will not let us go'.

This is the argument: We have a Christian hope that we are going to see and share the glory of God. We believe this hope is a sure hope; that it is 'no mockery'; that it will never disappoint us. We know this because God loves us—He will never let us down; He will never let us go.

'Ah, but', somebody says, 'how do you know that God loves you like that?' Paul gives us the answer to

this question, too. We know God loves us like that because we have an inner experience of it, because (NEB)
'God's love has flooded our inmost heart through the
Holy Spirit he has given us'. The Holy Spirit has been
given to every believer, and one of the works He does
is to pour out God's love—not our love for God, but
God's love for us—like a mighty flood into our hearts,
to make us vividly and inwardly aware that God loves
us. Or, as Paul expresses the same truth later, in 8 : 16,
'it is the Spirit himself bearing witness with our spirit
that we are children of God', and that He is our
heavenly Father who loves us. The Holy Spirit delights to pour into our hearts the love of God.

The change of tense in the verbs of verse 5 is worth
noting: the Holy Spirit *was given* to us (*dothentos*, an
aorist participle, referring to a past event); but God's
love *has been poured out* into our hearts (*ekkechutai*,
a perfect tense, referring to a past event with abiding
results). So we learn that the Holy Spirit was given to
us the moment we believed and were converted. At the
same time He flooded our hearts with the love of God.
He still does. The flood remains. The once-given Spirit
caused a permanent flood of divine love in our hearts.

Summing up these first five verses, then, the fruits
of justification are threefold: peace with God, the
enmity over; grace, as a state in which we stand; and
a hope (a 'joyful and confident expectation'—Grimm-
Thayer lexicon) of the glory of God at the end. This
hope is produced by the character which God is working in us through the endurance of suffering, but is
confirmed by the assurance of His love which the Holy
Spirit has given us. In other words, justification, which
is itself a momentary act, a judicial decision of our
righteous God who pronounces us righteous in Christ,
nevertheless leads on to a permanent relationship with

Himself, summed up in the words 'grace' now, and 'glory' at the end.

We come now to verses 6–11, in which the fruits of justification are further revealed. In verses 1–5 Paul joined peace and hope, justification and glorification, making *our* sufferings the link. In verses 6–11 he does it again, this time, however, making *Christ's* sufferings and death the link.

d. Christ died for the ungodly (verses 6–8)

Let us consider what Paul tells us about the death of Jesus. He reminds us that Christ died for the utterly undeserving. This is the emphasis of these verses. Just see the unflattering terms in which we are described. First of all, we are depicted as 'helpless' (verse 6), unable to save ourselves; secondly, we are called 'ungodly' (verse 6), because of our revolt against the authority of God; thirdly, we are called 'sinners' (verse 8), because we have missed the mark of righteousness, however carefully we may have aimed at it; and fourthly (verse 10), we are called 'enemies', because of the hostility between us and God. What a fearful, devastating description of man in sin! We are failures, we are rebels, we are enemies, and we are helpless to save ourselves.

Yet the thrust of these verses is that it is for *such* people that Jesus Christ died. We ourselves would 'hardly die for a righteous man' (verse 7)—somebody coldly upright in his conduct—'though perhaps for a good man'—warm and attractive in his goodness— some people would 'dare even to die'. 'But God shows *his* love for us (and "his" is emphatic in the Greek : He shows His own, His unique love) in that while we were yet sinners Christ died for us.' Not for the coldly upright, nor even for the warmly attractive and good, but for sinners, unattractive, unworthy, undeserving.

This provides the setting for the argument which follows in verses 9–11. It is an *a fortiori* or 'much more' argument, an argument from the lesser to the greater, which reaches up to a new truth by standing on the shoulders of an old one. What Paul does is this. He contrasts the two main stages of our salvation—justification and glorification—and he shows how the first is the guarantee of the second.

e. Justification and glorification contrasted (verses 9–11)

It is important to grasp the details of the comparison Paul makes.

First, he contrasts what they are. 'Since, therefore, we are now justified by his blood, much more shall we be saved by him from the wrath of God' (verse 9). The contrast in this verse is plain. It is between our present justification and our future salvation from the out-poured wrath of God on the Day of Judgment. If we have already been saved from God's condemnation because we are justified, then how much more shall we be saved from His wrath on that day? This is the first contrast.

Secondly, he contrasts how they are achieved. Verse 10 reads: 'If while we were enemies we were reconciled to God by the death of his Son, much more, now that we are reconciled, shall we be saved by his life.' Here the emphatic contrast concerns the means adopted to accomplish the two stages of salvation, namely, the death and the life of the Son of God. The 'life', of course, means the risen life of Christ. The risen life of Christ is going to complete in heaven what the death of Christ began on earth. I think the best commentary on this truth is found in Romans 8: 34, where we are told that Christ not only died but was raised; that He sits at the right hand of God and makes intercession for us, bringing to perfection by His life what He accomplished by His death.

Thirdly, he contrasts the people who receive them. Look at verse 10 again: 'If while we were enemies we were reconciled to God . . ., much more, now that we are (no longer enemies but) reconciled, shall we be saved. . . .' If God reconciled His enemies, He will surely save His friends.

There is therefore, in verses 9 and 10, a powerful argument that we are going to inherit a full and final salvation. There is a strong presumption that we shall never be allowed to fall by the way, but shall be preserved to the end and glorified. This is not just sentimental optimism; it is grounded upon irresistible logic. The logic of it is this, that if, when we were enemies, God reconciled us through giving His Son to die for us, how much more, now we are God's friends, will He finally save us from His wrath by His Son's life? If God performed the more costly service (involving His Son's death) for His enemies, He will surely perform the less costly service now that His erstwhile enemies are His friends. Meditate on this until you see the irrefutable logic of Paul's argument.

But there is more to the Christian life than this. Christianity is not just a matter of looking back to justification and on to glorification. The believer is not preoccupied always with the past and the future. He has a present Christian life to live as well, and so we read in verse 11, 'we also rejoice in God through our Lord Jesus Christ'. We rejoice in hope. We rejoice in sufferings also. But above all we rejoice in God Himself; and we do it through Jesus Christ.

As we have already seen, it is through Jesus Christ that we have peace with God (verse 1); it is through Jesus Christ that we have obtained access into this grace in which we stand (verse 2); it is through the blood of Christ that we have been reconciled (verse 9); it is through the life of Christ that we are going to be finally saved (verse 10); and it is through the same Lord Jesus Christ (verse 11) that we received (*elabomen*, an aorist) our reconciliation. So we rejoice in God through our Lord Jesus Christ, through the One who has achieved these priceless blessings for us.

Looking back over the first half of chapter 5, we see that in both its paragraphs (verses 1–5 and 6–11) the apostle's thought moves from justification to glorification, from what God has already done for us to what He is still going to do for us in the consummation. It comes out clearly in verses 1 and 2, 'Since we are justified by faith . . . we rejoice in our hope of sharing the glory of God'; and again in verse 9, 'Since, therefore, we are now justified by his blood, much more shall we be saved by him from the wrath of God.'

Further, in both parts, verses 1–5 and 6–11, Paul writes of the love of God and bases our assurance of final salvation upon it. There is no other assurance. In verse 5 he declares that God's love has flooded our hearts, and in verse 8 that 'God shows his love for us in that while we were yet sinners Christ died for us'. If we Christians dare to say that we are going to heaven when we die, and that we are sure of final salvation, as we do dare to say, it is not because we are self-righteous or self-confident; it is because we believe in the stead-fast love of God, the love that will not let us go.

Then, next, both parts provide some *ground* for believing that God loves us. These grounds are two, objective and subjective. The objective ground for believing that God loves us is historical. It concerns the death of His Son on the cross: 'Christ died for us

while we were yet sinners, and that is God's own proof
of his love towards us' (verse 8, NEB). The subjective
ground for believing that God loves us is experimental.
It is not in history but in experience. It concerns not
the death of Christ, but the gift of the Holy Spirit
within us. So we see in verse 8 that God proves His
love at the cross and in verse 5 that He has poured
His love into our hearts. This is how we know that
God loves us. We know it rationally as we contem-
plate the cross, where God gave His best for the worst.
And we know it intuitively as the Spirit floods our
hearts with a sense of it.

In each case the apostle links to this knowledge our
assurance of final salvation. Verse 5: 'hope does not
disappoint us.' That is, we know that our expectation
of final salvation will be fulfilled; it is well grounded
and will not deceive or disappoint us. How do we
know? Because the love of God has flooded our hearts
through the Holy Spirit. Verses 8–10: we know that
we are going to be saved from the wrath of God. How?
Because God proves His love for us by having given
His Son to die for us while we were enemies and
sinners.

Is there a Christian reading these pages who is full
of doubts about his eternal salvation? Are you sure
that you have been justified, but not at all sure that all
will be well in the end? If so, let me stress again that
final glorification is the fruit of justification. 'Those
whom he justified he also glorified', as we shall see
when we come to study Romans 8:30. If this is your
problem, I would urge you to trust in the God who
loves you. Look at the cross and accept it as God's own
proof that He loves you. Ask Him to go on flooding
your heart with His love through the indwelling
Spirit. And then away with gloomy doubts and fears!
Let them be swallowed up in the steadfast love of God.

II. THE MEDIATOR OF OUR JUSTIFICATION
(5:12-19)

*Therefore as sin came into the world through one man
and death through sin, and so death spread to all men
because all men sinned—sin indeed was in the world
before the law was given, but sin is not counted where
there is no law. Yet death reigned from Adam to
Moses, even over those whose sins were not like the
transgression of Adam, who was a type of the one who
was to come.*

*But the free gift is not like the trespass. For if many
died through one man's trespass, much more have the
grace of God and the free gift in the grace of that one
man Jesus Christ abounded for many. And the free
gift is not like the effect of that one man's sin. For the
judgment following one trespass brought condemnation, but the free gift following many trespasses brings
justification. If, because of one man's trespass, death
reigned through that one man, much more will those
who receive the abundance of grace and the free gift
of righteousness reign in life through the one man
Jesus Christ.*

*Then as one man's trespass led to condemnation for
all men, so one man's act of righteousness leads to
acquittal and life for all men. For as by one man's
disobedience many were made sinners, so by one man's
obedience many will be made righteous.*

In the first section Paul has traced our reconciliation
and our final salvation to the death of God's Son. His
exposition immediately prompts this question: but
how can one person's sacrifice have brought such
blessings to so many? It is not, in Sir Winston Chur-
chill's famous expression, that 'so many owe so much

to so few'. It is that so many owe so much to *one person*, Christ crucified. How can that be?

The apostle answers this anticipated question by drawing an analogy between Adam and Christ the 'second Adam'.[1] Both Adam and Christ demonstrate the principle that many can be affected (for good or ill) by one person's deed.

a. The history of man before Christ (verses 12–14)

The first three verses concentrate on Adam. 'As sin came into the world through one man and death through sin, and so death spread to all men because all men sinned——' (verse 12). This is a very important verse, summing up, as it does, in three stages the history of man before Christ. It tells us first, that sin entered into the world through one man; second, that

---

[1] It is fashionable nowadays to regard the story of Adam and Eve as 'myth', not history. But the Scripture itself will not allow us to do this. There may well be some figurative elements in the first three chapters of Genesis. We would not want to dogmatize, for example, about the precise nature of the seven days, the serpent, the tree of life or the tree of the knowledge of good and evil. But this does not mean we doubt that Adam and Eve were real people who were created good but fell through disobedience into sin. The best argument for the historicity of Adam and Eve is not scientific (*e.g.* the homogeneity of the human race), but theological. The biblical Christian accepts Adam and Eve as historical not primarily because of the Old Testament story, but because of New Testament theology. In Rom. 5 : 12–19 and 1 Cor. 15 : 21, 22, 45–49 the apostle draws an analogy between Adam and Christ which depends for its validity on the historicity of both. Each is presented as the head of a race—fallen humanity owing its ruin to Adam, and redeemed humanity owing its salvation to Christ. Death and condemnation are traced to Adam's disobedience, life and justification to Christ's obedience. The whole argument is built on two historical acts—the self-willed disobedience of Adam and the self-sacrificing obedience of Christ.

death entered into the world through sin, because
death is the penalty for sin; and third, that death
spread to all men because all men sinned (this is explained later). These are the three stages—sin, death
and universal death; so that the present situation of
universal death is due to the original transgression of
one man.

In verses 13 and 14 this progression (from one man
sinning to all men dying) is further explained. Death
is visited on all men today, not just because all men
have sinned like Adam, but because all men sinned *in*
Adam. And this is plain, Paul argues, because of what
happened during the time between Adam and Moses,
between the fall and the giving of the law. During that
period people certainly sinned, but their sins were not
reckoned against them because 'sin is not counted
where there is no law' (verse 13). Yet, although there
was then no law, these people still died. Indeed (verse
14) 'death reigned from Adam to Moses, even over
those whose sins were not like the transgression of
Adam'. So Paul argues, logically, that the reason why
they died is not because they deliberately transgressed
like Adam and died for their transgression, but because they and the whole of humanity (Christ only
excepted) were included in Adam, the head of the
human race. This embraces us. In biblical terminology
(*cf.* Heb. 7 : 10) we were 'still in the loins of' Adam,
and therefore in some sense involved in his sin. We
cannot point the finger at him in self-righteous inno-
cence, for we share in his guilt. And it is because we
sinned in Adam that we die today.

b. The analogy between Adam and Christ (verses 15–
19)
So far Paul has concentrated on Adam. At the end of
verse 14, however, he calls Adam 'a type of the one

who was to come'. That is, Adam was the prototype of Jesus Christ. And in verse 15 he begins to unfold the analogy between Adam and Christ. It is a fascinating and enthralling analogy, in which there is both similarity and dissimilarity. The similarity between the two lies in the pattern of events: the fact that many people have been affected by one man's deed. That is the *only* similarity between them. There are three differences: of motive, of effect and of nature, between Adam's one deed and Christ's one deed. The motive of the deed, the reason *why* Adam sinned, is different from the motive behind Christ's death. The effect of the deed, the result of Adam's sin, is different from the effect of Christ's death. The nature of the deed, what Adam did, is different from the nature of what Christ did. Let us look at these three separately.

1. *The motive.* At the beginning of verse 15 we read that 'the free gift is not like the trespass'. The trespass, or offence, was a deed of sin (the Greek word *paraptōma* means a fall or deviation from the path). Adam knew the path well enough. God had told him what path he should walk along, but he deviated from it and went astray. The free gift, on the other hand, is the Greek word *charisma*, which indicates that it was a deed of grace. We may therefore say that Adam's deed was one of self-assertion—that is *why* he did it; he wanted to go his own way. But Christ's deed was a deed of self-sacrifice, of free and unmerited favour. That, then, is the contrasting motive between the two deeds: self-will in the one instance and self-sacrifice in the other.

2. *The effect.* This we see in verses 15b–17. The reference to the contrasting results of the work of Adam and Christ is already anticipated at the end of verse 15, where we are told that the sin of one man brought to many the grim penalty of death, whereas

the grace of God and of the one Man Jesus Christ
abounded to many in bestowing a free gift, which
(according to 6:23) is eternal life. So death is contrasted with life, and the next two verses (16 and 17)
elaborate the opposite effects brought about by the
deeds of Adam and of Christ. 'The judgment following one trespass brought condemnation, but the free
gift following many trespasses brings justification. If,
because of one man's trespass, death reigned through
that one man, much more will those who receive the
abundance of grace and the free gift of righteousness
reign in life through the one man Jesus Christ.' Now,
without spending time on detail, let us just mark quite
clearly the contrasting effects of the deeds of Adam
and of Christ. The sin of Adam brought condemnation (*katakrima*); the work of Christ brings justification (*dikaiōma*). The reign of death is due to Adam's
sin; a reign of life is made possible through Christ's
work. The contrast could not be more complete. It is
in fact absolute: between condemnation and justification; between death and life.

It is worth noting in passing, however, the precise
way in which the apostle contrasts life and death. It is
not simply that the reign of death is superseded by a
reign of life, for (verse 17) it is not life which reigns,
but *we* who are said to 'reign in life'. Formerly death
was our king. Death reigned over us and we were its
subjects, slaves under its totalitarian tyranny. We do
not now exchange death's kingdom for another kingdom, so that we remain slaves and subjects although
in a different sense. No; once delivered from the rule
of death we begin ourselves to rule over death and all
the enemies of God. We cease to be subjects and become kings, sharing the Kingship of Christ.

3. *The nature.* We have seen that Adam's deed and
Christ's were different in their motive (what prompted

them) and in their effect (what resulted from them).
Now the apostle contrasts the two deeds themselves.
The parallel here (verses 18 and 19) is similar to what
has gone before, but the emphasis now is on precisely
what Adam did and what Christ did. According to
verse 18, what led to condemnation for all was one
man's offence, whereas what led to justification and
life for all who are in Christ is one man's righteousness. Adam's 'trespass' was a failure to keep the law.
Christ's 'act of righteousness' was a fulfilment of the
law. Verse 19 follows on from this: 'as by one man's
disobedience (*parakoē*) many were made sinners, so by
one man's obedience (*hupakoē*) many will be made
righteous.' There is the contrast, quite clearly, between the nature of the two deeds: Adam disobeyed
the will of God and so fell from righteousness; Christ
obeyed the will of God and so fulfilled all righteousness. *Cf.* Matthew 3:15 and Philippians 2:8.

We may thus briefly summarize the analogy drawn
between Adam and Christ. As to the motive for their
deeds, Adam asserted himself, Christ sacrificed Himself. As to the effect of their deeds, Adam's deed of sin
brought condemnation and death, Christ's deed of
righteousness brought justification and life. As to the
nature of their deeds, Adam disobeyed the law, Christ
obeyed it.

So then, whether we are condemned or justified,
whether we are spiritually alive or dead, depends on
which humanity we belong to—whether we belong to
the old humanity initiated by Adam, or to the new
humanity initiated by Christ. And this, in its turn,
depends on our relation to Adam and to Christ. We
need to get this quite clear: *all* men are in Adam,
since we are in Adam by birth, but not all men are in
Christ, since we can be in Christ only by faith. In

Adam by birth we are condemned and die. But if we are in Christ by faith we are justified and live.

This brings us back, in conclusion, to the privileges of the justified with which the chapter began, because these are ours only in and through Jesus Christ. Verse 1 declared: 'We have peace with God *through* our Lord Jesus Christ', and verse 2: '*Through him* we have obtained access to this grace in which we stand.' Peace, grace, glory (the three privileges of the justified) are not given to those who are in Adam, but only to those who are in Christ.

CHAPTER TWO

UNION WITH CHRIST

Romans 5:20—6:23

We have discovered from Romans 5 that peace with God—a continuing relationship of grace now and of glory in the world to come—is the first privilege of the believer. The second—unfolded in Romans 6—is his union with Christ, a state which leads to holiness.

The great theme of Romans 6, and in particular of verses 1–11, is that the death and resurrection of Jesus Christ are not only historical facts and significant doctrines, but personal experiences of the Christian believer. They are events in which we ourselves have come to share. All Christians have been united to Christ in His death and resurrection. Further, if this is true, if we have died with Christ and risen with Christ, it is inconceivable that we should go on living in sin.

Romans 6 in fact consists of two parallel sections (verses 1–14 and 15–23). Each elaborates the same general theme, that sin is inadmissible in a Christian. But the argument used in the two parts is slightly different. In verses 1–14 it is our union with Christ which is unfolded; in verses 15–23 it is our slavery to God. This is our position as Christians. We are one with Christ and we are slaves of God. The argument for holiness is grounded upon this double fact.

I. ONE WITH CHRIST (6:1–14)

What shall we say then? Are we to continue in sin that grace may abound? By no means! How can we who died to sin still live in it? Do you not know that all of us who have been baptized into Christ Jesus were baptized into his death? We were buried therefore with him by baptism into death, so that as Christ was raised from the dead by the glory of the Father, we too might walk in newness of life.

For if we have been united with him in a death like his, we shall certainly be united with him in a resurrection like his. We know that our old self was crucified with him so that the sinful body might be destroyed, and we might no longer be enslaved to sin. For he who has died is freed from sin. But if we have died with Christ, we believe that we shall also live with him. For we know that Christ being raised from the dead will never die again; death no longer has dominion over him. The death he died he died to sin, once for all, but the life he lives he lives to God. So you also must consider yourselves dead to sin and alive to God in Christ Jesus.

Let not sin therefore reign in your mortal bodies, to make you obey their passions. Do not yield your members to sin as instruments of wickedness, but yield yourselves to God as men who have been brought from death to life, and your members to God as instruments of righteousness. For sin will have no dominion over you, since you are not under law but under grace.

a. Objection from the critics

The chapter opens with two questions: 'What shall we say then? Are we to continue in sin that grace may abound?'

In order to understand what lies behind these questions, we need to glance back to the end of the previous chapter, particularly verses 20 and 21. Paul has been comparing and contrasting the work of Adam and the work of Christ. The parallel which he draws between them is so neat and tidy that there might seem to be no room in his scheme for one of the most important events occurring between Adam and Christ, namely the giving of the law through Moses. So, having described the entry of sin in verse 12, he now describes in verse 20 the entry of law (the verbs are similar).

Why was the law given? 'Law came in, to increase the trespass' (verse 20); and the law is said to have 'increased' sin because the effect of the law was to expose sin and even to provoke it (see the exposition of 7 : 7–12). As H. P. Liddon comments, 'Things had to become worse with the human family before they could be better.'

'But', the apostle continues, 'where sin increased, grace abounded all the more.' God's purpose in this was the establishment of His reign of grace. To explain and paraphrase verse 21 : just as in Old Testament days sin held sway, reigning through Moses' law and resulting in death, so God's will is that in New Testament days grace shall hold sway, reigning through Christ's righteousness and resulting in eternal life.

It is against this background that Paul now asks his questions : 'What shall we say then? Are we to continue in sin that grace may abound?' The fact that in the past increased sin brought increased grace (5 : 20, 21) prompts the question whether the same is not still true today. Could I not argue something like this : 'I have been justified freely by the grace of God. If I sin again, I shall be forgiven again, by grace. And the more I sin, the more opportunity grace will have to

express and exhibit itself in my forgiveness. So shall I
continue in sin that grace may abound?'

Now the apostle was giving expression to one of the
objections raised by his contemporaries against the
gospel of justification by grace alone, through faith
alone. They maintained that the doctrine of free grace
leads to antinomianism (lawlessness), that it weakens
our sense of moral responsibility and actually en-
courages us to sin. Critics objected to the gospel on
that ground in Paul's day, and the same ignorant
argument is frequently heard today.

If our acceptance before God depends entirely on
His free grace, irrespective of any works of ours, then
surely we may live as we please? If God 'justifies the
ungodly', which He does (Rom. 4 : 5) and indeed delights to do, there is no point in being godly; rather
the reverse. Thus the doctrine of justification by grace
is said to put a premium on sin. Some people evidently
did argue like this. Jude called them 'ungodly persons
who pervert the grace of our God into licentiousness
and deny our only Master and Lord, Jesus Christ'
(verse 4).

Paul's answer is one of outraged indignation : 'Are
we to continue in sin that grace may abound? By no
means!' Notice that Paul did not deny the doctrine to
which his critics took exception, but only their unwarranted deduction from it. He neither contradicted nor
withdrew, nor even modified his gospel of free salvation. Salvation *is* a free and unmerited gift! Indeed,
the fact that people could and did object to it in these
terms, and that Paul did not withdraw, proves con-
clusively that this is the gospel.

How then does Paul answer? After his emphatic
negative he counters his critics' question with another
question (verse 2). 'How can we who died to sin still
live in it?' In other words, there is in our critics' ob-

B

jection to justification by faith a fundamental misunderstanding of it, and so of what it means to be a
Christian. The Christian life begins with a death to
sin (the phrase is not that we 'are dead', AV, but that we
'died', an aorist tense). And in view of this it is ridicu-
lous to ask if we are at liberty to continue in sin. How
can we go on living in what we have died to?

The RSV and NEB are a little misleading in their
phrase 'how *can* we' continue in sin, as if Paul were
arguing the impossibility of it. In the Greek the verb
is just in the simple future tense. Literally translated it
would be, 'we died to sin (past); how *shall* we live in it
(in the future)?' It is not the literal impossibility of
sin, but the moral incongruity of it, which the apostle
is emphasizing. J. B. Phillips catches this rather well
in his translation, 'We, who have died to sin—how
could we live in sin a moment longer?'

The big question, however, is this, How and in what
sense have we 'died to sin'? Clearly we will not go on
living in what we have died to; but what does it mean
to have died to sin? How and when did it happen?
The apostle Paul takes the rest of the paragraph to
explain this and we shall follow him as he unfolds his
mighty argument step by step.

b. Paul's counter-argument

Step one: Christian baptism is baptism into Christ.
That is what he says in verse 3, 'Do you not know that
all of us who have been baptized into Christ Jesus
. . .?' That people can even think of asking whether
Christians are free to sin betrays a complete lack of
understanding of what a Christian is and what Christian baptism is. A Christian is not merely a justified
believer. He is someone who has entered into a vital
personal union with Jesus Christ. Indeed, properly
understood, justification itself is not a merely legal

pronouncement affecting our status without touching our life. We are justified 'in Christ' (Gal. 2 : 17, literally). There is no possibility of justification through Christ without union with Christ; the former depends on the latter.

And baptism signifies this union with Christ. Of course baptism has other meanings, including a washing from sin and the gift of the Holy Spirit. But essentially it signifies union with Christ. Again and again in the New Testament the preposition that is employed with the verb 'to baptize' is not 'in' (*en*) but 'into' (*eis*). In His great commission the risen Lord said that we were to baptize (literally) 'into the name of the Father and of the Son and of the Holy Spirit'. In Acts, believers in both Samaria and Ephesus were baptized 'into the name of the Lord Jesus' (8 : 16; 19 : 5, literally). Galatians 3 : 27 speaks of 'as many of you as were baptized into Christ'. And the preposition is just the same here : 'baptized into Christ Jesus'.

Baptism in the New Testament is a dramatic sacrament or ordinance. It indicates not just that God washes away our sin, not just that He gives us the Holy Spirit, but that by sheer grace He places us 'into' Christ Jesus. That is the essence of the Christian life, visibly signified in baptism. Not, of course, that the outward rite of baptism by itself secures our union with Christ. By no means. It is inconceivable that the apostle, having spent three chapters arguing that justification is by faith alone, should now shift his ground, contradict himself and make baptism the means of salvation. We must give the apostle Paul credit for a little consistency of thought. No, when he writes that we are 'baptized into Christ Jesus', he means that this union with Christ, invisibly effected by faith, is visibly signified and sealed by baptism. Nevertheless, the first point he assumes is that being a

Christian involves a personal, vital identification with Jesus Christ, and that this union with Him is dramatically set forth in our baptism. This is step one.

Step two: Baptism into Christ is baptism into His death and resurrection. 'Do you not know', says Paul (verses 3-5), 'that all of us who have been baptized into Christ Jesus were baptized into his death? We were buried therefore with him by baptism into death, so that as Christ was raised from the dead by the glory of the Father (probably meaning "by that splendid revelation of the Father's power", J. B. Phillips), we too might walk in newness of life. For if we have been united with him in a death like his, we shall certainly be united with him in a resurrection like his.' That is to say, if we condense the apostle's words, baptism into Christ is baptism into His death and resurrection. The tense of the verb 'shall be' in verse 5 is future only in relation to our death with Christ; there is no reference here to the resurrection of the body.

These verses probably allude to the pictorial symbolism of baptism. When baptisms took place in the open air in some stream, the candidate would go down into the water—whether he was then only partially or totally immersed really does not matter—and as he went down into the water, whether partially or totally, he would seem to be buried and then to rise again. His baptism would dramatize his death, his burial and his resurrection to a new life. 'In other words,' writes C. J. Vaughan in his commentary, 'our baptism was a sort of funeral.' A funeral; yes, and a resurrection from the grave as well.

This, then, is the second stage in the apostle's argument. A Christian, by faith inwardly and by baptism outwardly, has been united to Christ in His death and resurrection. We are not to think of ourselves as just united to Christ in some vague, general sense. We must be more particular than that. The only Jesus Christ with whom we have been identified and made one is the Christ who died and rose again. So we have actually shared, willy-nilly, by union with Christ, in His death and resurrection.

Step three: Christ's death was a death to sin and His resurrection was a resurrection to God. This section is a more difficult one to understand. In verses 6–11 Paul writes: 'We know that our old self was crucified with him so that the sinful body might be destroyed, and we might no longer be enslaved to sin. For he who has died is freed (literally, "has been justified", *dedikaiōtai*) from sin. But if we have died with Christ, we believe that we shall also live with him. For we know that Christ being raised from the dead will never die again; death no longer has dominion over him. The death he died he died to sin, once for all, but the life he lives he lives to God. So you also must consider yourselves dead to sin and alive to God in Christ Jesus.'

This needs careful thought. Verse 10 explains how we are to think of the death and resurrection of Christ with which we have been united: 'The death he died he died to sin . . . the life he lives he lives to God.' Now, what is this death to sin, the death which Christ died (verse 10), and the death which we have therefore died in Him (verse 2, 'we . . . died to sin', and verse 11, 'consider yourselves dead to sin')?

1. Death to sin: a misunderstanding. It is necessary in this instance to begin by being negative, to demolish before we can construct, because of a current misunderstanding. There is a popular view of the death to sin described in Romans 6 which cannot stand up to a careful examination but leads people to self-deception, to disillusionment, and even to despair. This interpretation runs as follows: when you die physically your five senses cease to operate. You can no longer touch, taste, see, smell or hear. You lose all power to feel or to respond to stimuli. Therefore, by analogy, the popular view continues, to die to sin is to become insensitive to it. It is to be as unresponsive to sin as a corpse to physical stimuli.

This view lends itself to illustration. I have heard it put like this. One of the signs of life is the ability to respond to a stimulus. As you are walking along a street, you may see a dog or a cat lying in the gutter. You cannot tell by looking at it whether it is alive or dead. But touch it with your foot and you will know. If it is alive there is an immediate reaction. It jumps up and runs away. But if it is dead there will be no response at all. It will just lie there without moving. So, according to this popular view, the fact that we 'died to sin' means that we become unresponsive to it. We become like dead men, and when the stimulus of temptation comes we neither feel it nor react to it. We are dead. And the reason for this, so we are told from verse 6, is that our old nature in some mystical way was actually crucified. Christ bore not only our guilt but our 'flesh', our fallen nature. It was nailed to the cross and killed, and our task (however much evidence we may have to the contrary) is to reckon it dead (verse 11).

Let me bring you some quotations which express this view. J. B. Phillips seems to hold it. He says that 'a dead man can safely be said to be immune to the power of sin' (verse 7) and that we are to look upon ourselves as 'dead to the appeal and power of sin', unresponsive to it. C. J. Vaughan writes, 'A dead man cannot sin. And you are dead. . . . Be in relation to all sin as impassive, as insensible, as immovable as is He who has already died.' H. P. Liddon comments, 'This *apothanein* (having died) has presumably made the Christian as insensible to sin as a dead man is to the objects of the world of sense.'

Despite all this, however, there are serious, indeed fatal, objections to this view. If we consider the matter carefully, we know that this is not the sense in which Christ died to sin; neither is it the sense in which we have died to sin.

It is of great importance to observe that the phrase 'died to sin' comes three times in this paragraph. Twice it refers to Christians (verses 2 and 11) and once it refers to Christ (verse 10). Now it is a fundamental principle of biblical interpretation that the same phrase recurring in the same context bears the same meaning. We must therefore find an explanation of this death to sin which is true both of Christ and of Christians. We are told that 'he died to sin', and that 'we died to sin'. So, whatever this death to sin is, it has to be true of the Lord Jesus and of us.

Take Christ and His death first. What does verse 10 mean by saying 'he died to sin, once for all'? It cannot mean He became unresponsive to it, because this would imply that He was formerly responsive to it. Was our Lord Jesus Christ at one time so alive to sin that He needed subsequently to die to it? And indeed was He so continuously alive to sin that He had to die to it decisively once and for all? Of course not. That would be intolerable.

Now how about ourselves and our death to sin? Have we died to sin in the sense that our old nature has become unresponsive to it? Again, No. A second vital principle of biblical interpretation is that you must explain the text within its context, the part in relation to the whole, and the special in the light of the general. So we ask: What is the general teaching

of the rest of Scripture about the old nature? It is that
the old nature is still alive and active in regenerate
believers. Indeed the context of this very text teaches
the same truth. In verses 12 and 13 the apostle says,
'Let not sin therefore reign in your mortal bodies, to
make you obey their passions. . . . Do not yield your
members to sin'—commands which would be entirely
gratuitous if we had so died to sin that we were now
unresponsive to it. And the rest of the Epistle to the
Romans confirms this. At the beginning of chapter 8
Paul urges us not to set our mind on the things of the
flesh and not to walk according to the flesh. In 13:14
he says we are not to make any provision for the flesh
to gratify its desires. These would be absurd injunc-
tions if the flesh were dead and had no desires. It is
these verses to which we must point those who, while
agreeing that they are not 'dead' or oblivious to the
allurements of the world, yet maintain that they have
a 'sanctified disposition' from which the inclination to
sin has been removed. But these instructions about
not gratifying or yielding to the lusts of the flesh show
that our temptations still come from within, not
merely from without, *i.e.* from the flesh, not just from
the world and the devil.

Besides, Christian experience proves that this is not
the correct interpretation. We must notice that the
apostle is not referring to a few exceptionally holy
Christians, who may have passed through some special
experience. He is describing all Christians who have
believed and been baptized into Christ: 'How can we
who died to sin still live in it? Do you not know that
all of us who have been baptized into Christ Jesus
were baptized into his death?' (verses 2, 3).

So this death to sin, whatever it is, is common to
every Christian. But are all baptized believers dead to
sin in the sense of being inwardly unresponsive to it?

Do they find that they have become insensible to it, that it lies quiescent within them, and that they can reckon it so? No. On the contrary, scriptural and historical biographies, and our own experience, combine to deny these ideas. Far from being dead in the sense of being quiescent, our fallen and corrupt nature is alive and kicking. So much so that we are exhorted not to obey its lusts; and so much so that we are given the Holy Spirit for the precise purpose of subduing and controlling it. And what would be the purpose of that if it were already dead?

What is more, I would add this: one of the real dangers of this popular view—as I know in my own experience, because I was taught it and once held it— is that when people have tried to reckon themselves dead in that sense (although knowing full well that they are not dead), they are torn between their interpretation of Scripture and their empirical experience. As a result, some of them begin to doubt the truth of God's Word, while others, in order to maintain their interpretation, resort even to dishonesty about their experience.

Let me sum up the objections to the popular view. Christ did not die to sin (in the sense of becoming insensitive to it) because He never was thus alive to it that He needed to die to it. We have not died to sin in this sense either, because we *are* still alive to it. Indeed, we are told to 'mortify' it, and how can you kill what is already dead? My intention in saying all this is not to attack the cherished views of other Christians or to hurt people's feelings, but to open up a new dimension of Christian living and to pave the way to a new liberty in what follows.

2. *Death to sin: Paul's real meaning*. What then is the meaning of this 'death to sin' which Christ died and which we have died in Him? How can we inter-

pret the expression in such a way that it is true of Christ and of Christians—*all* Christians? The answer is not far to seek.

The whole misunderstanding illustrates the great danger of arguing from an analogy. In every analogy (in which somebody is likened to something) we need to enquire carefully at what point the parallel or similarity is being drawn; we must not press a resemblance at every point. For instance, Jesus said we were to become like little children. He did not mean by this that we were to manifest every characteristic of children (including ignorance, waywardness, stubbornness and sin), but only one, namely humble dependence. In the same way, because we are said to have 'died' to sin, this does not necessarily mean that every characteristic of a dead man belongs to the Christian, including insensibility to stimuli. We have to ask ourselves: at what point is the analogy made? What is the meaning of 'death' in this context?

If we answer these questions from Scripture rather than from analogy, from biblical teaching about death rather than from the properties of dead men, we shall find immediate help. Death is thought of and spoken of in Scripture not so much in physical terms as in moral and legal terms; not as a state of lying motionless like a corpse but as the grim but just penalty for sin. Whenever sin and death are spoken of together in the Bible, the essential relationship between them is that death is sin's penalty. And this is true all through the Bible, from the second chapter in Genesis, where God says, 'In the day that you eat (and therefore sin) . . . you shall die', to the last chapters of the Revelation where we are told about that awful destiny of sinners which is called the 'second death'. Sin and death are linked in Scripture as an offence and its just reward. That is certainly true in the Epistle to the

Romans. In 1 : 32 we are told of God's decree that those who sin 'deserve to die', while we read in the last verse of this very chapter, 'The wages of sin is death' (verse 23). This, then, is how dying and death are to be understood. And this is the meaning of death which is true both of Christ and of Christians.

Take Christ first (verse 10). 'The death he died he died to sin, once for all.' What does this mean? It can mean only one thing; that Christ died to sin in the sense that He bore sin's penalty. He died for our sins, bearing them in His own innocent and sacred Person. He took upon Himself our sins and their just reward. The death that Jesus died was the wages of sin—our sin. He met its claim, He paid its penalty, He accepted its reward, and He did it 'once', once and for all. As a result sin has no more claim or demand on Him. So He was raised from the dead to prove the satisfactoriness of His sin-bearing, and He now lives for ever to God.

If this is the sense in which Christ died to sin, it is equally the sense in which we, by union with Christ, have died to sin. We have died to sin in the sense that in Christ we have borne its penalty. Consequently our old life has finished; a new life has begun.

Some may object that we surely cannot speak of *our* bearing the penalty of *our* sins in Christ, since we cannot die for our sins; He alone has done that. It has even been suggested to me that this is a veiled form of justification by works! But it is nothing of the kind. Of course Christ's sin-bearing sacrifice was altogether unique, and we cannot share in its offering. But we can and do share in its benefits by being in Christ. And the New Testament expresses this truth by saying not only that Christ died for us, but that we died in Christ. See, for example, 2 Corinthians 5:14, 15, where Paul argues that because 'one has died for all; therefore all have died' (*i.e.* in Him).

We return now to verse 6, which speaks of our death. It is in three parts. Something happened, in order that something else might happen, in order that something else might happen. Departing from the RSV text I would translate it like this: (1) 'We know that our old self was crucified with him'; (2) 'in order that the sinful body might be destroyed'; (3) 'in order that we might no longer be enslaved to sin'. There are three clear stages.

The ultimate stage is plain: 'that we might no longer be enslaved to sin'. And surely this is our heart's desire—to be delivered from the slavery and bondage of sin. It is the last thing mentioned in verse 6. How does it happen? We must look back to the two earlier stages which lead to this deliverance. The first is called the crucifixion of the old man, the second the destruction of the body of sin, and the second is dependent on the first. Indeed, our old man was crucified, we are told, in order that the body of sin might be destroyed, in order that we should no longer be enslaved to sin. It may be helpful to take these phrases in the opposite order.

First, the destruction of the body of sin. Now 'the sinful body' or 'the body of sin' (AV) is not the human body. This body is not sinful in itself. It means rather the sinful nature which belongs to the body. (See verse 12.) The NEB helpfully renders it 'the sinful self'. Now it is God's purpose, according to this verse, that the sinful self should be 'destroyed', so that we should no longer serve sin. The Greek verb (*katargēthē*) occurs again in reference to the devil in Hebrews 2:14. It means not to become extinct, but to be defeated; not to be annihilated, but to be deprived of power. Our old nature is no more extinct than the devil; but God's will is that the dominion of both should be broken. In fact, the sinful nature has been overthrown by something which happened on the cross, and which is described in the first phrase of verse 6.

This is the crucifixion of our 'old man' (AV) or our 'old self'. What is this 'old self'? It is not the old nature. How can it be if the 'body of sin' means the old nature? The two expressions cannot mean the same thing or the verse makes nonsense. No. The 'old self' denotes, not our old unregenerate nature, but our old unregenerate life—what the NEB calls 'the man we once were'. Not my lower self, but my former self. So what was crucified with Christ was not a part of me called my old nature, but the whole of me as I was before I was converted. My 'old self' is my pre-conversion life, my unregenerate self. This should be plain because in this chapter the phrase 'our old self was crucified' (verse 6) is equivalent to 'we . . . died to sin' (verse 2).

One of the causes of confusion regarding this verse is Paul's use of the word 'crucified'. Many people associate it in their minds with Galatians 5:24, where 'those who belong to Christ Jesus' are said to 'have crucified the flesh with its passions and desires'. A mental link between the two verses would naturally suggest that in Romans 6:6 Paul is alluding to the crucifixion of the 'flesh' or old nature. But the two verses are quite different. This should be clear because Romans 6:6 describes something which has happened to us ('our old self was crucified with him'), whereas Galatians 5:24 refers to something which we ourselves have done (we 'have crucified the flesh'). There are, in fact, two separate and distinct ways in which the New Testament speaks of the Christian's spiritual death in connection with holiness. The first is a death to sin, and the second a death to self. Our death to sin is through identification with Christ; our death to self is through imitation of Christ. First, we have been cruci-

fied with Christ; but then we not only have decisively
crucified (*i.e.* repudiated) the flesh with its passions
and desires, but we take up our cross *daily* and follow
Christ to crucifixion (Lk. 9:23). The first is a legal
death, a death to the penalty of sin; the second is a
moral death, a death to the power of sin. The first
belongs to the past, and is unique and unrepeatable: I
died (in Christ) to sin once. The second belongs to the
present, and is continuous and repeatable: I die (like
Christ) to self daily. It is with the first of these two
that Romans 6 is concerned.

We can now take the three stages of verse 6 in the
right order. First, our old self was crucified with
Christ; that is, *we* were crucified with Christ. We became identified with Him by faith and baptism, and
so we shared in His death to sin. We were thus crucified with Christ, secondly, in order that our sinful
nature might be deprived of its power. And this took
place, thirdly, in order that we should no longer be
enslaved to sin.

The question now is, How can this crucifixion with
Christ lead to an overcoming of the old nature, and
so to a deliverance from the bondage of sin? Verse 7
supplies the answer. It is because (lit.) 'he who has
died has been justified from his sin'. The AV and RSV
have taken an unwarranted liberty in translating the
Greek verb (*dedikaiōtai*) as 'freed'. It occurs fifteen
times in Romans, and twenty-five times in the New
Testament, and it always means 'justified'.

The only way to be justified from sin is to receive
the wages of sin. There is no other escape but to bear
its penalty. To illustrate this from the administration
of justice in our country: How can a man who has
been convicted of a crime and sentenced to a term of
imprisonment be justified? There is only one way. He

must go to prison, and pay the penalty of his crime. Once he has served his term, he can leave the prison justified. He need no longer fear the police or the law or the magistrates. The law no longer has anything against him, because he has paid the penalty of breaking it. He has served his sentence; he is now justified from his sin.

The same principle holds good if the penalty is death. There is no way of escape or justification except by paying the penalty. You may say that in this case to pay the penalty is no way of escape. And you would be right if we were talking about capital punishment on earth. Once a murderer has died (in countries where capital punishment survives), his life on earth is finished. He cannot live again on earth justified, like a man who has served a prison sentence. But the wonderful thing about our Christian justification is that our death is followed by a resurrection in which we can live the life of a justified person, having paid the death penalty (in Christ) for our sin.

For us, then, it is like this. We deserved to die for our sin. By union with Jesus Christ we did die—not in our own person (that would have meant eternal death) but in the Person of Christ our Substitute, with whom we have been made one by faith and baptism. And, by union with the same Christ, we have risen again to live the life of a justified sinner, a life that is altogether new. The old life is finished. We have died to it. The penalty is borne. We emerge from this death justified. The law cannot touch us, because the penalty of sin is paid.

With this in mind we can move on to verses 7–11. 'He who has died is freed (literally "has been justified") from sin. But if we have died with Christ, we believe that we shall also live with him. For we know that Christ being raised from the dead will never die again;

death no longer has dominion over him. The death he died he died to sin, once for all, but the life he lives he lives to God. So you also must consider yourselves dead to sin and alive to God in Christ Jesus.'

Let me put it in a rather more homely way. Suppose there is a man called John Jones, an elderly Christian believer, who is looking back upon his long life. His career is divided by his conversion into two parts, the old self—John Jones before his conversion—and the new self—John Jones after his conversion. The old self and the new self (or the 'old man' and the 'new man') are not John Jones' two natures; they are the two halves of his life, separated by new birth. At conversion, signified in baptism, John Jones, the old self, died through union with Christ, the penalty of his sin borne. At the same time John Jones rose again from death, a new man, to live a new life to God.

Now John Jones is every believer. We are John Jones, if we are in Christ. The way in which our old self died is that we were crucified with Christ. By faith and baptism we were united to Christ in His death. The death He died to sin became our death; its benefits were transferred to us. So, having died to sin with Christ, we have been justified from our sin (verse 7); and having risen with Christ we are alive, justified, to God (verses 8, 9). Our old life finished with the death it deserved. Our new life began with a resurrection. Christ died to sin once for all and lives to God continuously (verse 10). So we (verse 11), who are one with Christ, must reckon, *i.e.* realize, that we too have died to sin and live to God. This brings us to the fourth step.

Step four: Since we have died to sin and live to God, we must reckon it so. Let me put it in this way: If Christ's death was a death to sin (which it was), and if His resurrection was a resurrection to God (which it was), and if we have been united to Christ in His death and resurrection (which we have), then we ourselves have died to sin and risen to God; and we must reckon it so. 'So you also must consider yourselves (av "reckon . . . yourselves") dead to sin and alive to God in (that is, through union with) Christ Jesus' (verse 11).

Now 'reckoning' is not make-believe. It is not screwing up our faith to believe something we do not believe. We are not to pretend that our old nature has died when we know perfectly well that it has not. We are rather to realize that our old self—that is our former self—did die, thus paying the penalty of its sins and putting an end to its career. So Paul says 'reckon yourselves' (av), or better 'consider yourselves' (rsv), or better still 'regard yourselves' (neb), as being what in fact you are—dead to sin and alive to God. Once we realize that our old life has ended—the score settled, the debt paid, the law satisfied—we shall want to have nothing more to do with it.

I find it helpful to think in these terms. Our biography is written in two volumes. Volume one is the story of the old man, the old self, of me before my conversion. Volume two is the story of the new man, the new self, of me after I was made a new creation in Christ. Volume one of my biography ended with the judicial death of the old self. I was a sinner. I deserved to die. I did die. I received my deserts in my Substitute with whom I have become one. Volume two of my biography opened with my resurrection. My old life having finished, a new life to God has begun.

We are simply called to 'reckon' this—not to pretend it, but to realize it. It is a fact. And we have to lay hold of it. We have to let our minds play upon these truths. We have to meditate upon them until we grasp them firmly. We have to keep saying to ourselves, 'Volume one has closed. You are now living in volume two. It is inconceivable that you should reopen volume one. It is not impossible, but it is inconceivable.'

Can a married woman live as though she were still a single girl? Well, yes, I suppose she can. It is not impossible. But let her feel that ring on the fourth finger of her left hand, the symbol of her new life, the symbol of her identification with her husband, let her remember who she is, and let her live accordingly. Can a born-again Christian live as though he were still in his sins? Well, yes, I suppose he can. It is not impossible. But let him remember his baptism, the symbol of his identification with Christ in His death and resurrection, and let him live accordingly.

We need to keep reminding ourselves who we are and what we are. When Satan whispers in our ear, 'Go on. You sin. God will forgive you', and we are tempted to presume upon the grace of God, we are to say to him, in the words of verse 2, 'God forbid, Satan. I died to sin; how can I live in it? Volume one is closed. I am in volume two.' In other words, the apostle does not state the impossibility of sin in the Christian, but the utter incongruity of it. He asks the astonished, indignant question, 'How can we who died to sin still live in it?' To have died to sin and to live in it are logically irreconcilable.

So the secret of holy living is in the mind. It is in *knowing* (verse 6) that our old self was crucified with Christ. It is in *knowing* (verse 3) that baptism into Christ is baptism into His death and resurrection. It is in *reckoning*, intellectually realizing (verse 11), that in Christ we have died to sin and we live to God. We are to know these things, to meditate on them, to realize that they are true. Our minds are so to grasp the fact and the significance of our death and resurrection with Christ, that a return to the old life is unthinkable. A born-again Christian should no more think of going back to the old life than an adult to his childhood, a married man to his bachelorhood, or a discharged prisoner to his prison cell.

By union with Jesus Christ our whole status has changed. Our faith and baptism have severed us from the old life, cut us off from it irrevocably, and committed us to the new. Our baptism stands between us and the old life as a door between two rooms, closing upon the one and opening into the other. We have died. We have risen. How can we live again in what we have died to?

Step five: As those who are alive from the dead, we must not let sin reign within us, but yield ourselves to God. In verses 12–14 we have the negative and the positive set over against one another. First the negative: 'Let not sin therefore reign in your mortal bodies, to make you obey their passions' (verse 12); do not let sin be your king. 'Do not yield (or, do not go on yielding) your members to sin as instruments of wickedness' (verse 13a). That is, do not let sin rule you; and do not let sin use you (your members) in furthering its unrighteous purposes. Do not let sin be your king or your lord. Then the positive: Instead 'yield yourselves to God as men who have been brought from death to life' (verse 13b), which is precisely what you are. You have died to sin, bearing its penalty. You have risen again. You are alive from the dead. Now 'yield yourselves to God as men who have been brought from death to life, and your members to God as instruments of righteousness'. In other words, do not let sin be your king; let God be your king to rule over you. Do not let sin be your lord to use you in its service; let God be your lord to use you in His service.

Now why? What is the ground of this exhortation? What is the basic reason for yielding ourselves to God, and not to sin? The answer is, we are alive from the dead! We have died to sin, and we have risen to God. So we cannot yield ourselves to sin; we must yield ourselves to God. You see the irresistible logic of it, step by step? Because we are alive from the dead, sin shall not be our lord. Sin no longer has any business to be our lord, because now we are 'not under law, but under grace' (verse 14). God in grace has justified us in Christ. In Christ, sin's penalty is paid and the law's demands are met. Neither sin nor the law has any more claim upon us. We have been rescued from their tyranny. We have changed sides. Our status is new. We are no longer prisoners of the law, but children of God, and under His grace.

So it is that, to know that we are under grace, and not under law, far from encouraging us to continue in sin that grace may abound, actually weans us away from the world, the flesh and the devil. Because by grace we have opened a new volume of our biography, we cannot possibly reopen the first. Because by grace we are alive from the dead, we cannot possibly go back to the old life to which we have died.

II. SLAVES OF GOD (6:15-23)

What then? Are we to sin because we are not under law but under grace? By no means! Do you not know that if you yield yourselves to any one as obedient slaves, you are slaves of the one whom you obey, either of sin, which leads to death, or of obedience, which leads to righteousness? But thanks be to God, that you who were once slaves of sin have become obedient from the heart to the standard of teaching to which you were committed, and, having been set free from sin, have become slaves of righteousness. I am speaking in human terms, because of your natural limitations. For just as you once yielded your members to impurity and to greater and greater iniquity, so now yield your members to righteousness for sanctification.

When you were slaves of sin, you were free in regard to righteousness. But then what return did you get from the things of which you are now ashamed? The end of those things is death. But now that you have been set free from sin and have becomes slaves of God, the return you get is sanctification and its end, eternal life. For the wages of sin is death, but the free gift of God is eternal life in Christ Jesus our Lord.

The second half of the chapter (verses 15–23) is much less difficult than the first. It concerns not our union with Christ, but our slavery to God.

Notice that it begins in exactly the same way as the opening verses of the chapter. First comes a question: 'What then? Are we to sin because we are not under law but under grace?' (verse 15). This is the same question as in verse 1, 'What shall we say then? Are we to continue in sin that grace may abound?' This question is followed in verses 2 and 15 by the same answer, an emphatic negative, 'By no means!' or 'God forbid' (AV). Then comes another question explaining this negative and beginning 'Do you not know?' Verse 3: 'Do you not know that all of us who have been baptized into Christ Jesus were baptized into his death?' Similarly, verse 16: 'Do you not know that if you yield yourselves to any one as obedient slaves, you are slaves of the one whom you obey?'

It is worth getting the parallel clear in our minds, so that we grasp what it is Paul wants us to know. In verses 1–14 what we are to know is that through faith and baptism we are united to Christ, and therefore dead to sin and alive to God. In verses 15-23 what we are to know is that through self-surrender, through yielding ourselves, we are slaves of God and therefore committed to obedience. This is what the beginning of verse 16 says: Once you have chosen your master, you have no more choice but to obey. This is true as a principle, whether you yield to sin, ending in 'death', or to obedience, ending in 'righteousness', acceptance with God. In the next verses these two slaveries are contrasted: the slavery of sin and the slavery of God. The contrast is seen from their beginning, through their development, to their end.

Two slaveries contrasted (verses 17-22)

1. Their beginning (verses 17, 18). 'You who were once slaves of sin.' The tense of the verb is imperfect and suggests that this is what we are by nature, what we have always been. 'But . . . you . . . have become obedient (aorist tense) from the heart to the standard of teaching to which you were committed'—that is, the gospel. When the gospel was delivered to you, or you to it, you obeyed it from your heart. Paul's 'thank God' indicated that their response to the gospel was due to His grace. Our slavery to sin, then, began at our birth; it is our natural condition; but our slavery to God began when by grace we obeyed the gospel.

2. Their development (verse 19). 'I am speaking in human terms, because of your natural limitations. For just as you once yielded your members to impurity and to greater and greater iniquity, so now yield your members to righteousness for sanctification.' This shows that the result of the slavery of sin is the grim process of a moral deterioration, whereas the slavery of God results in the glorious process of a moral sanctification. Each slavery develops; neither stands still.

In one we get better and better, and in the other steadily worse.

3. *Their end* (verses 20–22). 'When you were slaves of sin . . . what return did you get from the things of which you are now ashamed ("you blush to remember"—J. B. Phillips)?' To this question there is no answer, for 'the end of those things is death'. So he goes on: 'But now that you . . . have become slaves of God, the return you get is sanctification and its end, eternal life.' Then verse 23 sums it up. Sin pays the wage we deserve, which is death, while God gives us a gift that we do not deserve, which is eternal life.

Here then are two completely different lives, lives totally opposed to one another—the life of the old self, and the life of the new. They are what Jesus termed the broad road that leads to destruction, and the narrow road that leads to life. Paul calls them two slaveries. By birth we are slaves of sin; by grace and faith we have become slaves of God. The slavery of sin yields no return, except a steady, moral deterioration and finally death. The slavery of God yields the precious return of sanctification and finally eternal life. The argument of this section, then, is that our conversion —this act of yielding or surrender to God—leads to a status of slavery, and slavery involves obedience.

CONCLUSION

'Shall we continue in sin?' That is the question with which both sections of this chapter began; a question posed by Paul's critics who intended by it to discredit his gospel; a question that has been asked ever since by the enemies of the gospel; a question that is often whispered in our ears by the greatest enemy of the gospel, Satan himself, who seeks to entice us into sin. As he asked Eve in the garden, 'Did God say . . .?', so he whispers in our ear, 'Why not continue in sin? Go on! You are under grace. God will forgive you.'

When this happens, how do we answer the devil? We must begin with an outraged negative, 'God forbid', 'By no means!' But then we need to go further and confirm this negative with a reason. And there is a reason, a solid, logical, irrefutable reason, why the subtle insinuations of the devil must be repudiated. It is most important, because it brings all this great theology down to the level of our practical everyday experience.

What is the reason we must give in rebutting the devil's enticements? It is based on what we are, namely that we are one with Christ (verses 1–14) and slaves of God (verses 15—23). We became united to Christ by baptism (at least outwardly and visibly). We became enslaved to God by the self-surrender of faith. But whether we emphasize the outward baptism or the inward faith, the point is the same. It is that our Christian conversion has had this result: it has united us to Christ, and it has enslaved us to God. This is what we are, every one of us: one with Christ, and a slave of God.

Further, what we are has these inescapable implications. If we are one with Christ (which we are), then with Christ we have died to sin and we live to God. If we are enslaved to God (which we are), then *ipso facto* we are committed to obedience. It is inconceivable that we should wilfully persist in sin, presuming upon the grace of God. The very thought is intolerable.

We need constantly to remind ourselves of these truths. We need to talk to ourselves about them, and ask ourselves, 'Don't you know?' . . . 'Don't you know that you are one with Christ? That you have died to sin and risen to God? Don't you know that you are a slave of God and therefore committed to His obedience? Don't you know these things?' And we must go on asking ourselves these questions until we reply, 'Yes, I *do* know, and by the grace of God I shall live accordingly.'

CHAPTER THREE

FREEDOM FROM THE LAW

Romans 7 : 1—8 : 4

INTRODUCTION

The third great privilege of the believer (unfolded in Romans 7) is freedom from the law.

But, someone may immediately object, how could freedom from the law possibly be regarded as a Christian privilege? Surely the law was the law of God and one of the Jew's most treasured possessions? In Romans 9 : 4 'the giving of the law' is included among the special favours bestowed upon Israel. To speak of the law in a derogatory fashion, or to hail deliverance from it as a Christian privilege, would seem to Jewish ears akin to blasphemy. The Pharisees were incensed against Jesus because they regarded Him as a law-breaker. As for Paul, a Jewish mob in the Temple precincts nearly lynched him because they believed he was 'teaching men everywhere against the people and the law and this place' (Acts 21 : 28).

What then was Paul's view of the law? Twice in Romans 6 he has written that Christians are 'not under law but under grace' (verses 14, 15). Such a statement must have sounded revolutionary to his readers. What on earth did Paul mean? Was God's holy law now abrogated? Could Christians afford to disregard it? Or had it some continuing place in the Christian life?

Such questions as these were no doubt commonplace

in the apostle's day. And they are by no means of merely antiquarian interest today, because the law of Moses was and is the law of God. If we are thoughtful Christians, we need to know what place God's law should occupy in our lives today. Besides, in recent days the whole subject has come to the fore again, in the debate over the New Morality. The New Moralist is a kind of twentieth-century antinomian—one who sets himself against the law. He declares that the category of law is altogether abolished in the Christian life, that the Christian has nothing to do with the law and that the law has nothing to do with the Christian. We shall therefore find that the somewhat intricate arguments, which the apostle develops in Romans 7, speak with real relevance to our contemporary situation.

Attitudes to the law

By way of introduction it may help us to find our way through this difficult chapter if we think of the three possible attitudes to the law—attitudes represented first by the legalist, secondly by the libertine or antinomian, and thirdly by the law-abiding believer.

1. The legalist is a man in bondage to the law. He imagines that his relationship to God depends on his obedience to it. And as he seeks to be justified by the works of the law, he finds the law a harsh and inflexible taskmaster. In Paul's vocabulary he is 'under the law'.

2. The antinomian (sometimes synonymous with 'libertine') goes to the other extreme. He rejects the law altogether, and even blames it for most of man's moral and spiritual problems.

3. The law-abiding believer preserves the balance. He recognizes the weakness of the law (Romans 8 : 3, 'God has done what the law, weakened by the flesh,

could not do'). The weakness of the law is that it can neither justify nor sanctify us, because in ourselves we are not capable of obeying it. Yet the law-abiding believer delights in the law as an expression of the will of God, and seeks by the power of the indwelling Spirit to obey it.

To sum up, the legalist fears the law and is in bondage to it; the antinomian hates the law and repudiates it; the law-abiding believer loves the law and obeys it.

Directly or indirectly, the apostle portrays each of these three characters in Romans 7. This is not to say he deliberately visualizes and addresses each of them in turn. But we can see their shadowy forms in this chapter as he overthrows the arguments of the legalist and the antinomian, and as he describes the conflict and the victory of the law-abiding believer.

The chapter in outline

It may help our understanding of the parts if we begin with a bird's-eye view of the whole chapter.

1. In verses 1–6 Paul asserts that the law no longer exercises lordship over us. We have been delivered from its tyranny by the death of Christ. Our Christian bondage is not to the law or to the letter of the law, but to Jesus Christ in the power of the Spirit. That is his message to the legalist.

2. In verses 7–13 he defends the law against the unjust criticisms of those who want to be rid of it altogether, and who blame the law for man's sorry state of sin (verse 7) and death (verse 13). Paul argues in this paragraph that the cause of our sin and death is not God's law, but our flesh, our sinful nature. The law itself is good (verses 12, 13). It is in our flesh that there dwells nothing good (verse 18). So it is quite mistaken and unfair to blame the law. That is his message to the antinomian.

3. Then in 7 : 14—8 : 4, he describes the inner conflict and the victory-secret of the believer. According to Galatians 5 the conflict is between 'the flesh' and 'the Spirit'. In this passage the terminology varies. Now it is between 'the mind' and 'the flesh'; now between 'the law of my mind' and 'the law of sin which dwells in my members'; and now between 'the law of the Spirit of life' and 'the law of sin and death'. It is summed up in 7 : 25, where 'I of myself' am said to be the servant of two masters. With my mind 'I . . . serve the law of God', I love it, and I want to keep it. But with my flesh, my old nature, 'I serve the law of sin'. That is, if I am left to myself, even as a Christian, I am a helpless captive, the slave of sin, and unable to keep the law. But (8 : 4) God has acted so that 'the just requirement of the law might be fulfilled in us, who walk not according to the flesh but according to the Spirit'. In other words, the Holy Spirit enables me to do what I cannot do by myself, even as a Christian. And that is Paul's message for the law-abiding believer.

I think it is important to notice the burden of the apostle's message to each of these three types. To the legalist, who is in bondage to the law, Paul emphasizes the death of Christ as the means by which we have been delivered from that bondage. To the antinomian, who blames the law, he emphasizes the flesh as being the prime cause of the law's failure, and of our consequent sin and death. To the law-abiding believer, who loves the law and longs to obey it, he emphasizes the indwelling of the Holy Spirit, as the God-appointed means by which alone the righteousness of the law can be fulfilled in us.

I am going to entitle verses 1–6 'the hardness of the law', because this is what the legalist fears, regarding the law as his lord and ignorant of his emancipation; verses 7–13 'the weakness of the law', because this is

what the antinomian does not understand, imagining
that its weakness is inherent, when actually it is in us
who cannot keep it; and 7 : 14—8 : 4 'the righteousness
of the law', because this is what is fulfilled in the
Spirit-led and law-abiding believer.

I. THE HARDNESS OF THE LAW (7 : 1–6)

Do you not know, brethren—for I am speaking to
those who know the law—that the law is binding on a
person only during his life? Thus a married woman is
bound by law to her husband as long as he lives; but
if her husband dies she is discharged from the law
concerning the husband. Accordingly, she will be
called an adulteress if she lives with another man
while her husband is alive. But if her husband dies she
is free from that law, and if she marries another man
she is not an adulteress.

Likewise, my brethren, you have died to the law
through the body of Christ, so that you may belong
to another, to him who has been raised from the dead
in order that we may bear fruit for God. While we
were living in the flesh, our sinful passions, aroused by
the law, were at work in our members to bear fruit for
death. But now we are discharged from the law, dead
to that which held us captive, so that we serve not
under the old written code but in the new life of the
Spirit.

Verse 1 begins: 'Do you not know, brethren . . .
that the law is binding on a person only during his
life?' The word for 'binding' is rendered in Mark
10 : 42 to 'lord it over', in the phrase 'those who are
supposed to rule over the Gentiles lord it over them'.
It speaks of the imperious authority or lordship of the
law over those who are subject to it.

The principle that Paul states in this first verse is one which, he says, would immediately be acknowledged by anybody who knows anything about law, whether Jewish or Roman. It is that the law is intended for the benefit of men on earth. It binds a person only during his lifetime. As an example of this general principle he chooses marriage, which is contracted between two persons until death parts them. Actually, the way Paul applies the principle of verse 1 presupposes an extension of it, namely that a law concerning a relationship between two people is binding only while *both* are alive. If either party dies, it ceases to operate. Thus in marriage, when one partner dies the other is free to marry again. Verses 2 and 3: 'a married woman is bound by law to her husband as long as he lives; but if her husband dies she is discharged from the law concerning the husband. Accordingly, she will be called an adulteress if she lives with another man while her husband is alive. But if her husband dies she is free from that law, and if she marries another man she is not an adulteress.' In the one case a married woman lives with another man and 'incurs the stigma of adultery' (J. B. Phillips), while in the other case she marries another man and she is not an adulteress. What makes the difference? Why does one remarriage make her an adulteress and the other not? The answer is simple: the second marriage is legitimate only if death has terminated the first. Death has released her from the law governing her former relationship, and so set her free to marry again.

After the principle (verse 1), and the illustration (verses 2, 3), comes the application (verses 4–6). It is this: just as death terminates a marriage, so death has terminated our bondage to the law. Verse 4: 'Likewise, my brethren, you have died to the law through the body of Christ, so that you may belong to another,

to him who has been raised from the dead in order
that we may bear fruit for God.'

It was 'the body of Christ' that died on the cross,
but through faith-union with Him we have shared
His death. Having been united with Jesus Christ
through faith, it may be said that *we* 'have died . . .
through the body of Christ'. And since we have died,
death has removed us altogether out of that sphere in
which the law exercises lordship. The dread penalty
for sin, prescribed by the law has been borne—by
Christ in our stead, or by us in Christ. Therefore, because the demands of the law have been met in the
death of Christ, we are no longer under the law, but
under grace.

In the husband–wife relationship it is the death of
one which renders the other free to marry again. In
the Christian life it is our own death (in Christ) which
sets *us* free to marry again. We who were bound to the
law have now died to it. So now we are free to be
joined to Christ, with whom we not only died but rose
again, in order to 'bear fruit for God'. In the old life
the fruit we bore was for death (verse 5); in the new
we bear fruit for God.

What is plain in these verses so far is that becoming
a Christian involves a complete change of relationship
and allegiance. At the end of chapter 6 it was two
slaveries set in contrast; here the Christian's position
is like two marriages, the first being dissolved by death,
and so permitting the second to take place. We were,
so to speak, 'married' to the law (our obligation to
obey it was as binding as a marriage contract). But
now we have been set free to marry Christ. It is a most
remarkable illustration of the marriage metaphor, to
indicate the reality and intimacy of our union with
Jesus Christ.

That brings us to verses 5 and 6. Having contrasted

the two marriages and their results (verse 4), Paul now contrasts the place of the law in them. Verse 5 describes our pre-conversion life ('while we were living in the flesh'), and verse 6 our new life ('but now . . .'). In the old life, the law was the means of arousing our sinful passions, and they led to our death. 'But now', verse 6, 'we are discharged from the law, dead to that which held us captive.'

Notice in verse 5 the complex of words which belong together—'flesh', 'sin', 'law' and 'death'. Our sinful passions originate in the flesh, are aroused by the law, and end in death. But now we have been liberated from the law and its provocation.

If we are discharged from the law, what next? Take careful note of this: emancipation from the law does not mean that we are now free to do as we please. Far from it. Freedom from the law spells not licence but another kind of bondage: 'so that' (verse 6) we are slaves. We are indeed free from the law—but free to serve, not to sin. And our new Christian slavery is (literally) not in oldness of letter but in newness of spirit. This is the familiar contrast (found *e.g.* in 2 Corinthians 3:6) between the old covenant and the new, between the law and the gospel. The old was a 'letter', an external code written upon stone tablets outside us; the new covenant, the gospel, is 'spirit', for the Holy Spirit writes God's law in our heart. This is our new bondage.

Before we leave this section we must look again at the question, Is the law still binding upon the Christian? The answer to that is, No and Yes! 'No' in the sense that our acceptance before God does not depend on it. Christ in His death fully met the demands of the law, so that we are delivered from it. It no longer has any claims on us. It is no longer our lord. 'Yes' in the sense that our new life is still a bondage. We still

C

'serve'. We are still slaves, although discharged from the law. But the motive and the means of our service have altered.

Why do we serve? Not because the law is our master and we have to, but because Christ is our husband and we want to. Not because obedience to the law leads to salvation, but because salvation leads to obedience to the law. The law says, Do this and you will live. The gospel says, You live, so do this. The motive has changed.

How do we serve? Not in oldness of letter, but in newness of spirit. That is, not by obedience to an external code, but by surrender to an indwelling Spirit.

Let me sum up this argument. We are still slaves. The Christian life is still a bondage of a kind. But the Master we serve is Christ, not the law. And the power by which we serve is the Spirit, not the letter. The Christian life is serving the risen Christ in the power of His indwelling Spirit.

II. THE WEAKNESS OF THE LAW (7:7-13)

What then shall we say? That the law is sin? By no means! Yet, if it had not been for the law, I should not have known sin. I should not have known what it is to covet if the law had not said, 'You shall not covet.' But sin, finding opportunity in the commandment, wrought in me all kinds of covetousness. Apart from the law sin lies dead. I was once alive apart from the law, but when the commandment came, sin revived and I died; the very commandment which promised life proved to be death to me. For sin, finding opportunity in the commandment, deceived me and by it killed me. So the law is holy, and the commandment is holy and just and good.

Did that which is good, then, bring death to me?

By no means! It was sin, working death in me through what is good, in order that sin might be shown to be sin, and through the commandment might become sinful beyond measure.

Verse 5 seemed to make the law responsible for our sins and our death: 'While we were living in the flesh, our sinful passions, aroused by the law, were at work in our members to bear fruit for death.' The apostle now defends the law against such an unjust criticism to which he may have seemed to lay himself open. Notice his questions in verses 7 and 13: 'What then shall we say? That the law is sin?' (verse 7). And 'Did that which is good (*i.e.* the law), then, bring death to me?' (verse 13). In other words, is God's law responsible for my sin and my death? Let us look at these two questions and at Paul's answers to them.

a. Is the law sin? (verses 7-12)

If we need to be delivered from the law in order to bear fruit for God (verse 4), does not this imply that the law is responsible for our sinful behaviour? Paul's answer is a categorical 'By no means!' And he proceeds in the next verses to show the relation between the law and sin. The law, he says, does not create sin. If you are a sinner it is not the law's fault. The relation between sin and the law is threefold.

1. The law reveals sin. Verse 7: 'If it had not been for the law, I should not have known sin. I should not have known what it is to covet if the law had not said, "You shall not covet."' So too Romans 3:20, 'through the law comes knowledge of sin'.

2. The law provokes sin. It not only exposes it, but actually stimulates and arouses it, as we have already seen in verse 5. Verse 8: 'Sin, finding opportunity (the word is used of a military base, a spring-board for

offensive operations) in the commandment, wrought
in me . . .'. This is what the law does. It actually provokes us to sin. Now the way in which the law does
this is a matter of everyday experience. Anyone who
has driven on one of the motorways will be familiar
with the peremptory traffic sign that says, 'Reduce
speed now'. And if I am not greatly mistaken the in-
stinctive reaction of many of us is, 'Why should I?'
That is the reaction that a law provokes in us. Or
again, when we read a prohibition on a door, 'Do not
enter', 'Private', we immediately want to do what is
forbidden us, because the commands and prohibitions
of the law provoke us to the opposite. That is what
Paul found with the tenth commandment prohibiting
covetousness: 'Sin, finding opportunity in the commandment, wrought in me all kinds of covetousness.'
So the law exposes sin and it provokes sin.

3. The law condemns sin. Verse 8b: 'Apart from
the law sin lies dead. I was once alive apart from the
law, but when the commandment came, sin revived
and I died (that is, I fell under the judgment of the
law); the very commandment which promised life
proved to be death to me. For sin, finding opportunity
in the commandment, deceived me and by it killed
me.' Here the apostle may well be relating his own
early experiences, how in childhood he was ignorant
of the law's demands, and so 'in the absence of law'
(NEB) was spiritually alive; but how later, maybe as a
boy of thirteen (the age when a Jewish boy took on
him the obligations of the law and became a 'son of
the commandment'), in his own graphic words (verse
9, NEB), 'when the commandment came, sin sprang to
life and I died' (under the law's judgment). Or he may
be summarizing the history of man, how God gave
the law to reveal sin, even to provoke and increase it,
and so to condemn it. At all events, the very law that

promised life (saying, 'Do this and you shall live'—
see Lv. 18:5) brought spiritual death to Paul, and.
using the commandment as a base of operations, both
deceived and killed him.

These, then, are the three devastating results of the
law: it reveals, provokes and condemns sin. But the
law is not in itself sinful. Nor does the law in itself
cause men to sin. It is 'sin', our sinful nature, which
uses the law to make men sin, and so to bring them to
ruin. In itself (verse 12) 'the law is holy, and the commandment is holy and just and good'.

The teaching of this paragraph is well summarized
by the question of verse 7 and the affirmation of verse
12. Verse 7: 'What then shall we say? That the law is
sin?' Verse 12: 'the law is holy, and the commandment is holy and just and good.' This brings us to the
second question.

b. Does the law then bring death? (verse 13)

It is quite true (verse 10) that 'the very commandment which promised life proved to be death to me'.
But is Paul saying that the law itself is guilty of
offering life with one hand and inflicting death with
the other? 'Are we to say then' (NEB), 'that this good
thing was the death of me?' Is it the law's fault that I
die? And again the apostle's answer is an emphatic
'By no means!' Verse 13: 'It was sin, working death
in me *through* what is good . . .'. Indeed, the 'ex-
ceeding sinful' (AV) nature of sin is seen in the way it
exploits a good thing (the law) for evil purposes. But
we cannot blame the law for this; we must blame sin.

Let me illustrate this. Take a criminal today. A
man is caught red-handed perpetrating some crime,
some breach of the law. What happens? He is arrested,
brought to trial, found guilty and sentenced to imprisonment. As he languishes in his prison cell, he is

tempted to blame the law for his imprisonment. And it is quite true that the law has convicted him and the law has sentenced him. But in reality he has no one to blame but himself and his own criminal offence. He is in prison because he has committed a crime. Of course the law has condemned him for doing it, but he cannot blame the law; he has only himself to blame.

Thus Paul exonerates the law. The law exposes sin, provokes sin, condemns sin. But the law cannot be held responsible for either our sins or our death. To quote Professor F. F. Bruce, 'The villain of the piece is *sin*'—that is, indwelling sin, the flesh, which is aroused by the law. These antinomians who say our whole problem is the law are quite wrong. Our real problem is sin, not the law. It is thus indwelling sin, our 'flesh' or fallen nature, which explains the weakness of the law to save us. The law cannot save us, for the simple reason that we cannot keep it; and we cannot keep it because of indwelling sin.

III. THE RIGHTEOUSNESS OF THE LAW
(7:14—8:4)

We know that the law is spiritual; but I am carnal, sold under sin. I do not understand my own actions. For I do not do what I want, but I do the very thing I hate. Now if I do what I do not want, I agree that the law is good. So then it is no longer I that do it, but sin which dwells within me. For I know that nothing good dwells within me, that is, in my flesh. I can will what is right, but I cannot do it. For I do not do the good I want, but the evil I do not want is what I do. Now if I do what I do not want, it is no longer I that do it, but sin which dwells within me.

So I find it to be a law that when I want to do right, evil lies close at hand. For I delight in the law of God,

in my inmost self, but I see in my members another
law at war with the law of my mind and making me
captive to the law of sin which dwells in my members.
Wretched man that I am! Who will deliver me from
this body of death? Thanks be to God through Jesus
Christ our Lord! So then, I of myself serve the law of
God with my mind, but with my flesh I serve the law
of sin.

There is therefore now no condemnation for those
who are in Christ Jesus. For the law of the Spirit of life
in Christ Jesus has set me free from the law of sin and
death. For God has done what the law, weakened by
the flesh, could not do: sending his own Son in the
likeness of sinful flesh and for sin, he condemned sin
in the flesh, in order that the just requirement of the
law might be fulfilled in us, who walk not according
to the flesh but according to the Spirit.

We have considered the hardness of the law, its un-
bending demands, from which we have been delivered
by the death of Christ, so that we are not under the
law any longer. We have considered the weakness of
the law, which lies not in itself, but in us, in our flesh.
We come next to the righteousness of the law, because
now we are to see how the Christian believer first delights in the law in his mind, and then fulfils its
righteousness by the power of the indwelling Spirit.

a. The question of Paul's experience

Before we look at the text in detail, there is an important question to be considered. Let me approach it
this way. There are two changes in the section beginning with verse 14.

1. A change of tense in the verbs. In the previous
paragraph (7–13) the verbs are predominantly in the
past tense (aorists), and they thus appear to refer to

Paul's past experience. Thus, 'sin sprang to life and I died' (verse 9, NEB); 'sin . . . killed me' (verse 11); 'Did that which is good, then, bring death to me? By no means! It was sin . . .' (verse 13). These are all verbs in the past tense. But now from verse 14 onwards the verbs are in the present tense, and thus seem to refer to Paul's present experience. Verse 14: 'I am carnal.' Verse 15: ' I do not do what I want, but I do the very thing I hate'—present tenses.

2. A change of situation. In the previous paragraph Paul describes how sin sprang to life through the law and killed him; it finished him off. But in this paragraph he describes his fierce continuing conflict with sin, in which he refuses to admit defeat, but is an active combatant.

Now these two changes seem at once to suggest that what Paul is portraying in verses 7–13 is his pre-Christian life, and in verses 14ff. his life as a Christian. Some commentators (from the Greek Fathers onwards) have rejected this view. They cannot conceive how a believer, let alone a mature believer like Paul, could describe his Christian experience in terms of such a fierce conflict—and indeed a conflict which he finds he cannot win. They argue therefore that this paragraph must describe Paul's pre-Christian conflict.

Yet there are two traits in the apostle Paul's self-portrait in this paragraph (14ff.) which led the Reformers, and have led most reformed commentators since, to be sure that these verses are actually the self-portrait of Paul the Christian. The first is his opinion of himself, and the second is his opinion of the law.

1. *Paul's opinion of himself.* What is this? Verse 18: 'I know that nothing good dwells within me, that is, in my flesh.' Verse 24: 'Wretched man that I am!' —and he cries out for deliverance. Now who but a mature Christian believer thinks and talks of himself

like that? The unbeliever is characterized by self-righteousness, and would never acknowledge himself a 'miserable creature', which is the NEB version of 'wretched man'. The immature believer is characterized by self-confidence, and does not ask who is going to deliver him. Only the mature believer reaches the place both of self-disgust and of self-despair. It is he who recognizes with limpid clarity that in his flesh dwells nothing good. It is he who acknowledges his wretchedness and appeals with faith for deliverance. So much for Paul's opinion of himself.

2. *Paul's opinion of the law.* First of all, he calls God's law 'good' (verse 16) and 'the good I want' (verse 19). That is, he acknowledges that the law is good in itself, and he longs with all his being to obey it. Again, in verse 22, he says, 'I delight in the law of God, in my inmost self.' This is certainly not the language of the unbeliever. The unbeliever's attitude to the law is given us in Romans 8 : 7, namely that 'the flesh', our unredeemed human nature, 'is hostile to God; it does not submit to God's law, indeed it cannot'. Here, however, far from being hostile to the law of God, Paul says that he actually loves it. Paul's hostility is reserved for what is evil. It is this he says he hates, while what is good he loves and delights in.

From these two points we deduce that the speaker in the last part of chapter 7 is a mature, believing Christian; a believer who has been given a clear and a proper view both of his own sinful flesh and of God's holy law. His position is that in his flesh there is nothing good, whereas God's law is the good that he desires. This is summed up in verse 14: 'The law is spiritual; but I am carnal.' We need to note the fact that 'the law is spiritual'. We must never set the law and the Spirit in opposition to one another as if they were contradictory. They are not. The Holy Spirit writes the law in our hearts. What Paul contrasts with the indwelling Spirit is not the law itself but 'the letter', that is, the law viewed merely as an external code. Now let me repeat that anyone who acknowledges the spirituality of God's law and his own natural carnality is a Christian of some maturity.

If this is so, however, why does Paul describe his experience in terms not only of conflict but of defeat? Why does he say not only that he wants to do good, but that he does not and cannot do it? The simple answer, surely, is this. In the previous paragraph (verses 7–13) he has shown that as an unbeliever he could not keep the law. In this paragraph (verses 14ff.) he shows that even as a Christian believer *by himself* he still cannot keep the law. He can recognize the goodness of the law, he can delight in the law, and he can long to keep the law, none of which was possible to him as an unbeliever. But the flesh, his fallen nature, which was his undoing before his conversion, leading him to sin and death, is still his undoing after his conversion—unless the power of the Holy Spirit subdues it (which is what he comes to later, in chapter 8). Indeed, an honest and humble acknowledgment of the hopeless evil of our flesh, even after the new birth, is the first step to holiness. To speak quite plainly, some of us are not leading holy lives for the simple reason that we have too high an opinion of ourselves. No man ever cries aloud for deliverance who has not seen his own wretchedness. In other words, the only way to arrive at faith in the power of the Holy Spirit is along the road of self-despair. No device exists to settle this issue for good. The power and subtlety of the flesh are such that we dare not relax one moment. The only hope is unremitting vigilance and dependence.

So both paragraphs, 7–13 and 14ff., emphasize that (whether we are believers or unbelievers, regenerate or unregenerate) indwelling sin, the flesh, is our big problem and is responsible for the weakness of the law to help us.

b. The text in detail

Verses 14-20. It is helpful to see that in this paragraph Paul says precisely the same thing twice over, no doubt for emphasis; first in 14-17, and then again in 18-20. These two sections are almost exactly parallel. So it may be best to look at them together.

1. Each section begins with a frank acknowledgment of our condition, of what we are in ourselves and of what we know ourselves to be.

Verse 14: 'We know that', although the law is spiritual, 'I am carnal (the flesh still indwelling me and exerting its influence upon me), sold under sin' (NEB, 'the purchased slave of sin'). That is what I am, even as a Christian, in myself. The flesh dwells in me and assaults me, and I am no match for it. Rather, in myself, and if left to myself, I am its slave, its reluctant, resistant slave.

Verse 18 also begins with what I 'know'. 'I know that nothing good dwells within me, that is, in my flesh.'

This, then, is what I know (because the Holy Spirit has shown it me) about myself: that the flesh still dwells in me, that no good dwells in it, and that, even as a Christian, if I am left to myself it brings me into captivity.

2. Each section continues with a vivid description of the resulting conflict.

Verse 15, NEB: 'I do not even acknowledge my own actions as mine.' That is, I do things against my will, things to which as a Christian I do not give my consent. The NEB goes on, 'for what I do is not what I want to do, but what I detest'.

Verses 18 and 19 reinforce this: 'I can will what is right (and I do will it), but (in myself) I cannot do it. For I do not do the good I want, but the evil I do not want is what I do.'

Let me stress again that this is the conflict of a Christian man, who knows the will of God, loves it, wants it, yearns to do it, but who finds that still *by himself* he cannot do it. His whole being (his mind and his will) is set upon the will of God and the law of God. He longs to do good. He hates to do evil—hates it with a holy hatred. And if he does sin, it is against his mind, his will, his consent; it is against the whole tenor of his life. Herein lies the conflict of the Christian.

3. Each section ends with a conclusion (couched in identical words) about the cause of a Christian's personal, moral inability apart from the Holy Spirit.

In verses 16 and 17 Paul says, 'Now if I do what I do not want'—if my situation can be summed up in the words 'I want, but I can't'—then clearly it is not the law's fault if I misbehave, because 'I agree that the law is good'. It is not even 'I that do it', because I do not do it voluntarily, but rather against my will; 'it is . . . sin which dwells within me'.

In verse 20 he gives the same conclusion, 'Now if I do what I do not want, it is no longer I that do it, but sin which dwells within me.'

We may summarize the teaching of these two parallel sections thus. First comes our condition: I know myself to be indwelt by the flesh, which contains no good but (if I am left to myself) holds me captive. Next the resulting conflict: I cannot do what I want, but I do do what I detest. Finally the conclusion: if my actions are thus against my will, the cause is sin which dwells within me. All along, what Paul is seeking to do is to expose the no-goodness of our flesh, to convince us that only the Holy Spirit can deliver us.

Verses 21–25. In this section the apostle takes the argument a stage further. He has been giving a plain description of his condition and conflict. Now he expresses it as a philosophy, in terms of 'laws' or principles at work in his situation. The general principle is set out in verse 21 : 'I find'—this is a sort of philosophical conclusion from my experience—'I find it to be a law (or, "I discover this principle", NEB) that when I want to do right, evil lies close at hand.'

This general principle is now (in verses 22, 23) broken down into two separate laws, principles or forces which are in opposition to each other. Verse 23 names them as 'the law of my mind' and 'the law of sin'. 'The law of my mind' is that 'I delight in the law of God, in my inmost self' (verse 22). 'The law of sin' is a principle or power 'in my members' which Paul describes as being 'at war with the law of my mind and making me captive' to itself. 'The law of my mind' is a force *'in my inmost self'*, my mind and my will, that simply loves the law of God. But 'the law of sin' is a force *'in my members'*, in my flesh, which hates the law of God. This is the philosophy of Christian experience. Our experience is that the good we want we do not do, while the evil we hate we do; the philosophy behind it is two laws in conflict, the law of my mind and the law of sin. Or, more simply, my mind and my flesh, my renewed mind and my old, unrenewed, unrenewable flesh. This conflict is a real bitter, unremitting battle in every Christian's experience : his mind simply delighting in God's law and longing to do it, but his flesh hostile to it, and refusing to submit to it (as in 8:7).

It is this conflict which leads us repeatedly to utter two apparently contradictory cries : 'Wretched man that I am! Who will deliver me . . .?' (verse 24) and 'Thanks be to God through Jesus Christ our Lord!'

(verse 25). The first is a cry of despair, the second a cry
of triumph. But both are the ejaculations of a mature
believer, who bemoans his inner corruption of nature
and longs for deliverance, and who exults in God
through Jesus Christ as the one and only Deliverer.
Moreover, the deliverance he longs for is not just self-
control here and now; it is also deliverance 'out of (as
the Greek preposition means) this body of death',
when he dies, and especially when he is clothed with
a new and glorious body on the last day.

I do not myself believe that the Christian ever, in
this life, passes for good and all out of the one cry
into the other, out of Romans 7 into Romans 8, out of
despair into victory.[1] No. He is always crying for deliverance, and he is always exulting in his Deliverer.
Whenever we are made conscious of the desires and
depravity of our fallen nature, and of the irreconcilable conflict between our mind and our flesh, we long
to be rid of indwelling sin and corruption, and we cry
out: 'Wretched man that I am (for that is what we are
and always will be)! Who will deliver me from this
body of death?' But then at once we answer our own
anguished question, and with a cry of triumph thank
our God for His mighty salvation. For we know that
He is the One who can subdue our flesh now by His
Spirit; and He is the One who on the last day, at the
resurrection, will give us a new body, set free from
indwelling sin.

Now in the last verse (25) Paul sums up with beauti-

---

[1] Those who believe that God's purpose for us is to exchange the conflict of Romans 7 for the victory of Romans 8
must find the last sentence of chapter 7 a big stumbling-block,
for immediately after the cry of exultant thanksgiving Paul
reverts to the conflict and concludes with a summary of it:
'So then, I of myself serve the law of God with my mind, but
with my flesh I serve the law of sin.'

ful lucidity the double servitude to which the Christian is liable; with my mind—with all my heart and soul, we might say—I serve the law of God, but with my flesh—until, and unless, it is subdued by the Spirit —I serve the law of sin. But no man can serve two masters simultaneously, and whether I serve the law of God or the law of sin depends on whether my mind or my flesh is in control. So the question now is, How can the mind gain ascendency over the flesh?

That brings us to the beginning of chapter 8 and to the gracious ministry of the Holy Spirit who in the latter part of chapter 7, although never far away in the background, has not once been named. This is in fact the progression of thought from Romans 7 to Romans 8. The conflict at the end of Romans 7 is between my mind and my flesh. The conflict at the beginning of Romans 8 is between the Holy Spirit and the flesh, the Holy Spirit coming to my rescue, allying Himself with my mind, the renewed mind He has given me, and subduing my flesh. It is the same conflict, but it is differently viewed and it has a different outcome. According to 7:22, the believer *delights in* the law of God, but in himself cannot carry it out because of indwelling sin. According to 8:4, however, he not only delights in, but actually *fulfils* the law of God because of the indwelling Spirit.

Chapter 8:1-4. In verses 1 and 2 the apostle steps back and surveys the whole Christian landscape. He portrays together the two great blessings of salvation which we have if we are 'in Christ Jesus'. 'In Christ Jesus' (verse 1) there is no condemnation. 'In Christ Jesus' (verse 2) 'the law of the Spirit of life (or the life-giving Spirit) . . . has set me free from the law of sin and death.' In other words, salvation belongs to those who are in Christ Jesus (who are vitally united to Him

by faith), and salvation is deliverance from both the
condemnation and the bondage of sin. Further, when
the apostle writes that there is no condemnation for
those in Christ *because* the Spirit has set us free from
the law, he is not making our sanctification the cause
or ground of our justification; but rather its necessary
fruit. It is as if he is saying: 'We know that in Christ
we are no longer condemned but justified, because in
Christ we have also been set free.' The two belong
inseparably together.

But how is this twofold salvation made available to
us? Verses 3 and 4 tell us. In verses 1 and 2 the scope
of salvation is stated: no condemnation, no bondage.
In verses 3 and 4 the way of salvation is unfolded: we
are told how God effects it.

Indeed, the first thing to note is that *God* has done
it. Notice verse 3: 'God has done what the law, weakened by the flesh, could not do.' We have seen all
along that the law's impotence is not intrinsic. Its
weakness is not in itself, but in us, because of our flesh.
Because of our flesh, we cannot keep the law. And
because we cannot keep it, it cannot save us. It can
neither justify nor sanctify us. So 'God has done what
the law, weakened by the flesh, could not do'.

How has He done it? He has done it through His
Son (verse 3) and through His Spirit (already named
in verse 2, and now again in verse 4). Through the
death of His incarnate Son God justifies us; through
the power of His indwelling Spirit He sanctifies us.

We must now look more closely at this marvellous
ministry of God's Son and of God's Spirit.

First (verse 3), God sent His Son, 'his own Son'. 'In
the likeness of sinful flesh' is a significant expression.
Not 'in sinful flesh', because the flesh of Jesus was sinless. Nor 'in the likeness of flesh', because the flesh of
Jesus was real. But 'in the likeness of sinful flesh',

because the flesh of Jesus was both sinless and real. God also sent His Son 'for sin'. The words (*peri hamartias*) may be general, indicating that He came to deal with the problem of sin. Or they may be specific and refer to His death 'as a sin offering' (RSV margin), since they frequently bear this sense in the Greek Old Testament.

The way in which Jesus Christ died 'as a sacrifice for sin' (NEB) is explained in the remarkable phrase which follows: 'he (God) condemned sin in the flesh.' That is, in the flesh of Jesus—real flesh, sinless flesh, yet made sin with our sins (2 Cor. 5:21)—God condemned sin. He condemned our sins in the sinless flesh of His Son who bore them.

And why did He do it? Not just that we might be justified (although indeed 'there is . . . now no condemnation for those who are in Christ Jesus' precisely because in Christ Jesus God condemned sin), but rather (verse 4) 'in order that the just requirement of the law might be fulfilled in us, who walk not according to the flesh but according to the Spirit'. This verse is of very great importance for our understanding of the Christian doctrine of holiness. It teaches us at least three major truths:

1. That holiness is the purpose of Christ's incarnation and death. We are specifically told that God sent His Son in the likeness of sinful flesh (the incarnation) and condemned sin in the flesh (the atonement), *in order that* the righteousness of the law might be fulfilled in us. God condemned sin in Christ, so that holiness might appear in us.

2. That holiness consists in the righteousness, the 'just requirement', of the law. This is what it is called in verse 4, which is therefore one of the most uncomfortable verses in the New Testament for the 'New Moralists' who say that the category of law is abol-

D

ished for the Christian. Far from being abolished, God
sent His own Son for this purpose, that its righteousness might be 'fulfilled' in us. Thus law-obedience,
which is not and cannot be the ground of our justification, is seen to be its fruit.

3. That holiness is the work of the Holy Spirit, for
'the just requirement of the law' is fulfilled in us *only*
when we 'walk . . . according to the Spirit'. We have
seen that nearly the whole of Romans 7 is devoted to
the theme that we cannot keep the law because of 'the
flesh'. Therefore, the only way to fulfil the law is to
'walk not according to the flesh but according to the
Spirit', by His power and under His control.

These three vital truths about Christian holiness tell
us why we should be holy, what holiness is, and how it
may be attained. The reason for holiness is the coming
and the death of Christ. The nature of holiness is the
righteousness of the law, conformity to God's will
expressed in His law. And the means of holiness is the
power of the Holy Spirit.

In summing up, we must glance back over this long
and intricate passage which we have been studying
(7 : 1—8 : 4). I entitled it 'Freedom from the law'. I
might equally have called it 'Fulfilment of the law',
because the passage teaches both truths. It began
(7 : 1–6) with a statement of the Christian's discharge
from the law (verse 6, 'now we are discharged from the
law'). It ends (8 : 4) with a statement of the Christian's
obligation to keep it ('that the just requirement of the
law might be fulfilled in us'). Moreover, both our discharge and our obligation are attributed to the death
of Christ (7 : 4; 8 : 3, 4)! 'But this is an intolerable
contradiction', someone may say. 'How can I be at the
same time both free from the law and obliged to keep
it?' The paradox is not hard to resolve. We are set free

from the law as a way of acceptance, but obliged to keep it as a way of holiness. It is as a ground of justification that the law no longer binds us (for our acceptance we are 'not under law but under grace'). But as a standard of conduct the law is still binding, and we seek to fulfil it, as we walk according to the Spirit. To understand what this means, and how to walk according to the Spirit, we must now study the next section of Romans 8.

CHAPTER FOUR

LIFE IN THE SPIRIT

Romans 8 : 5–39

Our fourth Christian privilege is life in the Spirit. So
far the Holy Spirit has not figured prominently in
these chapters. He is not named at all in chapter 6. He
is mentioned only once in chapter 5, as the One
through whom God's love has flooded our hearts (verse
5). And once only in chapter 7, where it is written that
our Christian bondage is not to an external code, but
an indwelling Spirit (verse 6). Now, however, in chapter 8, the Holy Spirit comes to the fore.

The Christian life, the life of a justified believer, is
seen as being essentially life in the Spirit, that is to say,
a life which is animated, sustained, directed and en-
riched by the Holy Spirit. The ministry of the Spirit in
this chapter is portrayed particularly in four areas.
First, in relation to our flesh, our fallen nature.
Secondly, in relation to our sonship, our adoption to
be the sons of God. Thirdly, in relation to our final
inheritance, including the redemption of our bodies on
the last day. Fourthly, in relation to our prayers, in
which we have to acknowledge our weakness.

The Holy Spirit's gracious activity in these four
areas may be summed up as follows : He subdues our
flesh (verses 5–13); He witnesses to our sonship (verses
14–17); He guarantees our inheritance (verses 18–25);
and He helps our weakness in prayer (verses 26, 27).
The chapter ends (verses 28–39) with an affirmation,

unsurpassed in grandeur, that the purposes of God are invincible and that the people of God are therefore absolutely and eternally secure.

I. THE MINISTRY OF THE HOLY SPIRIT (8:5-27)

For those who live according to the flesh set their minds on the things of the flesh, but those who live according to the Spirit set their minds on the things of the Spirit. To set the mind on the flesh is death, but to set the mind on the Spirit is life and peace. For the mind that is set on the flesh is hostile to God; it does not submit to God's law, indeed it cannot; and those who are in the flesh cannot please God.

But you are not in the flesh, you are in the Spirit, if the Spirit of God really dwells in you. Any one who does not have the Spirit of Christ does not belong to him. But if Christ is in you, although your bodies are dead because of sin, your spirits are alive because of righteousness. If the Spirit of him who raised Jesus from the dead dwells in you, he who raised Christ Jesus from the dead will give life to your mortal bodies also through his Spirit which dwells in you.

So then, brethren, we are debtors, not to the flesh, to live according to the flesh—for if you live according to the flesh you will die, but if by the Spirit you put to death the deeds of the body you will live. For all who are led by the Spirit of God are sons of God. For you did not receive the spirit of slavery to fall back into fear, but you have received the spirit of sonship. When we cry, 'Abba! Father!' it is the Spirit himself bearing witness with our spirit that we are children of God, and if children, then heirs, heirs of God and fellow heirs with Christ, provided we suffer with him in order that we may also be glorified with him.

I consider that the sufferings of this present time are

*not worth comparing with the glory that is to be re-
vealed to us. For the creation waits with eager longing
for the revealing of the sons of God; for the creation
was subjected to futility, not of its own will but by the
will of him who subjected it in hope; because the
creation itself will be set free from its bondage to
decay and obtain the glorious liberty of the children
of God. We know that the whole creation has been
groaning in travail together until now; and not only
the creation, but we ourselves, who have the first fruits
of the Spirit, groan inwardly as we wait for adoption as
sons, the redemption of our bodies. For in this hope we
were saved. Now hope that is seen is not hope. For who
hopes for what he sees? But if we hope for what we do
not see, we wait for it with patience.*

*Likewise the Spirit helps us in our weakness; for we
do not know how to pray as we ought, but the Spirit
himself intercedes for us with sighs too deep for
words. And he who searches the hearts of men knows
what is the mind of the Spirit, because the Spirit intercedes for the saints according to the will of God.*

a. The Spirit subdues our flesh (verses 5-13)

Verse 4, which we considered in the last chapter, says
that 'the just requirement of the law' can be fulfilled
in us believers only if we 'walk not according to the
flesh but according to the Spirit', following His
promptings and yielding to His control. Now the
apostle Paul explains why this is so. A great deal of it
has to do with our mind. Our walk depends on our
mind, our conduct on our outlook. As a man 'thinketh
in his heart (or mind), so is he' (Proverbs 23 : 7, AV) and
so he behaves. It is our thoughts, ultimately, which
govern our behaviour.

That is what the apostle writes in verse 5. 'For', he
says—and this is the reason why we can fulfil the law

only if we walk according to the Spirit—'those who live (literally, "are") according to the flesh set their minds on the things of the flesh, but those who live according to the Spirit set their minds on the things of the Spirit'. Now to 'set the mind upon' the flesh or the Spirit means to occupy ourselves with the things of the flesh or the Spirit. It is a question of our preoccupations, the ambitions which compel us and the interests which engross us; how we spend our time, money and energy; what we give ourselves up to. That is what we set our minds on.

Verse 6 describes the results of these two outlooks: 'To set the mind on the flesh', he says, 'is death.' Not it will be, but it is—now—death, because it leads to sin and so to separation from God, which is death. But 'to set the mind on the Spirit is life . . .'—now—because it leads to holiness and so to continuing fellowship with God, which is life. Further, it brings not only life, but 'peace': peace with God, which is life; and peace within ourselves, integration, harmony. Many of us would pursue holiness with far greater zeal and eagerness if we were convinced that the way of holiness is the way of life *and peace*. And that is precisely what it is; there is life and peace no other way.

By contrast, to set the mind on the flesh brings death *and war*. Verses 7 and 8: 'the mind that is set on the flesh is hostile to God; it does not submit to God's law, indeed it cannot; and those who are in the flesh cannot please God.' They 'cannot please God' because the only way to please Him is to submit to His law and obey it. Thus the mind of the flesh is hostile to God's law and will not submit to it, while the mind of the Spirit is friendly to God's law and delights in it.

Here, then, are two categories of people (those who are in the flesh, and those who are in the Spirit), who have two mentalities or outlooks (called the mind of the flesh and the mind of the Spirit), which lead to two patterns of conduct (walking according to the flesh and walking according to the Spirit), and result in two spiritual states (death and life). If we are in the flesh we set our mind on the things of the flesh, we walk according to the flesh, and so die. But if we are in the Spirit we set our mind on the things of the Spirit, we walk according to the Spirit, and so live. What we are governs how we think; how we think governs how we behave; and how we behave governs our relation to God—death or life. Once more, then, we see how much depends on our mind, where we set it, how we occupy it, and on what we focus and concentrate its energies.

That brings us to verse 9, in which the apostle applies personally to his readers the truths which he has so far expounded in general terms. He has just written (verse 8), '*those* who are in the flesh cannot please God.' Now (verse 9) he says, 'But *you* are not in the flesh, you are in the Spirit, if the Spirit of God really dwells in you. Any one who does not have the Spirit of Christ does not belong to him.' Notice the synonyms in this verse. First, the 'Spirit of God' and the 'Spirit of Christ'. Secondly, to be in the Spirit, and to have the Spirit dwelling in us. This is simply two ways of looking at the same experience. Thirdly, to have the Spirit dwelling in us (verse 9), and to have Christ dwelling in us (verse 10), are the same thing.

Quite apart from these instructive synonyms, verse 9 is of great importance. It tells us plainly that *the* distinguishing characteristic of the true Christian, which sets him apart from all unbelievers, is that the Holy Spirit dwells in him. Twice in chapter 7, in verses 17 and 20, the apostle has written of the 'sin which dwells within me'. But now he writes of the Spirit who dwells in us. Indwelling sin is the lot of all the children of Adam; the great privilege of the children of God is to have the indwelling Spirit to fight and subdue indwelling sin. And 'any one who does not have the Spirit of Christ does not belong to him'.

Verses 10 and 11 indicate the great consequence of having the Spirit dwelling in us. Both verses begin similarly with an 'if' clause. Verse 10: 'if Christ is in you . . .'. Verse 11: 'If the Spirit of him who raised Jesus from the dead dwells in you . . .'. What is the result of having Christ by His Spirit indwelling us? The answer is 'life'—life for our spirits now and life for our bodies at the end—because the Holy Spirit is the Spirit of life. He is the Lord, the life-giver. Thus verse 10: 'If Christ is in you, although your bodies are dead because of sin, your spirits are alive because of righteousness.' That is, although our bodies are prone to death, mortal, yet our spirits are alive, for the Holy Spirit has given them life. Because of Adam's sin we die physically; because of Christ's righteousness we live spiritually.

Further, although at present it is only our spirits which live (our bodies are mortal and must die), yet on the last day our bodies will live also. Verse 11: 'If the Spirit of him who raised Jesus from the dead dwells in you, he who raised Christ Jesus from the dead will give life to your mortal bodies also through his Spirit which dwells in you.' Notice the reference to the three Persons of the Trinity. The God who raised Christ from the dead will raise us, raise our bodies. Why? Because the Spirit dwells in them and thus hallows them. How? By the power of the same Spirit who indwells them. So the Holy Spirit, who has already given life to our spirits, will in the end give life to our bodies too.

'So then, brethren,' verse 12, 'we are debtors, not to the flesh, to live according to the flesh——', and the apostle breaks off before completing the sentence. If he had completed it, almost certainly he would have said that we are debtors to the Spirit, to live according to the Spirit.

This idea of being 'debtors' to the Holy Spirit is an interesting and compelling one. It indicates that we have an obligation to holiness. It is an obligation to be what we are, to live up to our Christian status and privilege, and to do nothing which contradicts it. In particular, if we *live* in the Spirit, we have an obligation to *walk* according to the Spirit.

This is the argument. If the Holy Spirit is our life-giver and dwells within us, we cannot possibly walk according to the flesh, because that way lies death. Such an inconsistency between what we are and how we behave, between possessing life and courting death, is unthinkable. We are alive! Our spirits are alive. The Holy Spirit has given us life. Therefore we are debtors to the Spirit who has given us life. And by His power we must put to death anything that threatens this new life, especially 'the deeds of the body'. It is only by their death that we shall live, that is, continue to enjoy the life which the Holy Spirit has given us.

Such is the solemn alternative of verse 13. 'If you let the flesh live,' Paul says, 'allowing it to prosper and flourish, the real you will die. But if you kill the deeds of the body, mortifying them or putting them to death, the real you will live.' And each of us has to choose between this way of life and this way of death. But Paul's point is that our choice is not really in doubt. 'We are debtors'; under obligation to make the right choice. If the Spirit has given life to our spirits, then we *must* put the deeds of the body to death, so that we may continue to live the life which the Spirit has given us.

Looking back over the paragraph, we can see something of the apostle's progression of thought. The essential background is that there are two categories of people—those who are in the flesh (the unregenerate) and those who are in the Spirit (the regenerate). 'Now you', he writes to the Romans (verse 9), 'belong to the latter category. You are not in the flesh but in the Spirit if, as I believe, the Spirit of God dwells in you. Further (verse 10), because Christ dwells in you by His Spirit, you are alive.'

Now these two facts are the incontrovertible, inescapable facts about every Christian. First, we have the Holy Spirit dwelling in us, and secondly, as a result, our spirits are alive because the Spirit has quickened us. Therefore, we are debtors (because of what we are) not to the flesh but to the Spirit. We are under a most solemn obligation to be what we are, to conform our conduct to our character, to do nothing inconsistent with the life of the Spirit within us, but rather to nourish this life and to foster it.

More specifically, if we are to be honourable and to discharge our debt, we shall be involved in two processes. The theological names for these are 'mortification' and 'aspiration'—words which express the proper attitude to adopt towards the flesh on the one hand, and the Spirit on the other. We must put to death the deeds of the body or flesh, which is mortification. And we must set our mind on the things of the Spirit, which is aspiration.

Mortification (putting to death by the power of the Spirit the deeds of the body) means a ruthless rejection of all practices we know to be wrong; a daily repentance, turning from all known sins of habit, practice, association or thought; a plucking out of the eye, a cutting off of the hand or foot, if temptation comes to us through what we see or do or where we go. The only attitude to adopt towards the flesh is to kill it.

Aspiration (setting our mind on the things of the Spirit) is a whole-hearted giving of ourselves, in thought and energy and ambition, to 'whatever is true and honourable, just and pure, lovely and gracious' (see Phil. 4:8). It will include a diligent use of the 'means of grace', such as prayer, Bible reading, fellowship, worship, the Lord's Supper, and so on. All this is involved in setting our mind upon the things of the Spirit.

Both mortification and aspiration are expressed by verbs in the present tense, because they are attitudes to be adopted and then constantly, unremittingly maintained. We are to keep putting to death the deeds of the body ('If any man would come after me, let him deny himself and take up his cross *daily* and follow me'). We are to keep setting our mind on the things of the Spirit. Then there is something else mortification and aspiration have in common. Both hold the secret to life, in the fullest sense. There is no true life without the death called mortification, and there is no true life without the discipline called aspiration. It is while we put to death the deeds of the body that we shall *live* (verse 13); it is while we set our minds on the things of the Spirit that we find *life* and peace (verse 6). So the Holy Spirit subdues the flesh as we mortify it in His power, and as we set our minds upon the things of the Spirit.

b. *The Spirit witnesses to our sonship* (verses 14–17)

The emphasis on the work of the Spirit continues in this paragraph, but our Christian status and privilege are now described in different terms. What the apostle has just said (verse 13) is, 'if by the Spirit you put to death the deeds of the body you will live'. What he now says (verse 14) is, 'all who are led by the Spirit of God are sons of God'. The two sentences are closely parallel. Both refer to the activity of the Spirit, but the first in terms of life, the second in terms of sonship.

What visions of intimacy with God the word 'sonship' conveys! Access to God and fellowship with God as Father—these are the privileges of His children. Not all human beings are God's children, however. Verse 14 definitely and deliberately limits this status to those who are being led by the Spirit, who are being enabled by the Spirit to walk along the narrow path of righteousness. To be led by the Spirit and to be sons of God are virtually convertible terms. All who are led by the Spirit of God are the sons of God, and therefore all who are sons of God are led by the Spirit of God.

This is made even clearer in the next verse (15) which refers to the kind of Spirit we received (aorist tense, referring to our conversion), not a Spirit of slavery, but of adoption or sonship. The Holy Spirit (who is given to us when we believe) makes us sons, not slaves. He does not recall us to the old slavery spoiled by fear. He gives us a new sonship in which we approach God as our Father. More than that, He goes on to assure us of the status which He brings us. Verses 15b and 16: 'When we cry, "Abba! Father!"' —the very words the Lord Jesus Himself used in intimate prayer to God—'it is the Spirit himself bearing witness with our spirit that we are children of God.' This rsv rendering shows that the inner witness of the Spirit is given us when we pray. It is in our access to God in prayer that we sense our filial relationship to Him and know ourselves the children of a heavenly Father. And when our spirit is in communion with God, the Holy Spirit bears witness with our spirit (so that there are two concurrent witnesses) that we are indeed God's children.

Verse 17: 'and if children, then heirs, heirs of God and fellow heirs with Christ, provided we suffer with

him in order that we may also be glorified with him.'
Once more, as in chapter 5, suffering is the pathway to
glory. And notice that it is 'with Christ'. The whole
Christian life is identification with Christ. If we share
His Sonship, we shall share His inheritance in glory;
but if we are to share His glory, we must share His
suffering first.

c. The Spirit guarantees our inheritance (verses 18-25)

The theme of this paragraph is the contrast between
present suffering and future glory that Paul mentioned
in verse 17. He begins (verse 18) by saying that the
two are not to be compared; they are rather to be contrasted, because future glory will far surpass all present
suffering. This he proceeds to elaborate in a magnifi-
cent, cosmic setting. For in the rest of the paragraph
he goes on to show how both in present suffering and
in future glory the whole creation and the new creation, the church, are involved together. The two
creations (old and new, physical and spiritual, nature
and the church) suffer together now and are going to
be glorified together in the end. As nature has shared
in man's curse (Genesis 3), and now shares in man's
tribulation, so it will come to share in man's glory.
Verse 19: 'the creation waits with eager longing', as
if on tiptoe with expectation, 'for the revealing of the
sons of God', because that is the time when it too will
be redeemed.

1. *The creation* (verses 19-22). The creation (NEB
'the created universe') is mentioned four times, once in
each verse. Notice how its present sufferings are described. Verse 20: it 'was subjected to futility, not of
its own will but by the will of him who subjected it in
hope'. Verse 21: it is held in 'bondage to decay'. Verse
22: it 'has been groaning in travail together until
now'. 'Futility' in verse 20 means 'frustration' (NEB). It

is the word that is translated 'vanity' in the Greek version of Ecclesiastes and C. J. Vaughan writes, 'The whole Book of Ecclesiastes is a commentary upon this verse'. 'Vanity of vanities, says the Preacher . . . All is vanity.' This futility or frustration, to which God has subjected nature, is explained in the next verse (21) as a 'bondage to decay', the continuous cycle of birth, growth, death and decomposition, the whole process of deterioration in a universe that appears to be running down. Further, this process is (whether literally or metaphorically) accompanied by pain. Futility, decay and pain; these are the words which the apostle uses to depict the present suffering of nature.

But it is only temporary, for the present sufferings of nature will lead to a future glory. In each verse this is stressed. Verse 20: if the creation has been subjected to vanity, it has been thus subjected 'in hope', that is, with a view to a brighter future. Verse 21: 'the creation itself will be set free from its bondage to decay and obtain the glorious liberty of the children of God.' Bondage will give place to liberty; decay or corruption to glory incorruptible. If we are to share Christ's glory (verse 17), creation is going to share ours. Then in verse 22 the groans and pains of the creation are likened to the pangs of childbirth. In other words, they are not meaningless or purposeless pains, but pains necessarily experienced in the bringing to birth of a new order (cf. Mt. 24:8).

2. *The church* (verses 23–25). We move now from the creation to the church, which is the new creation of God. Observe the transition from the one to the other. Verse 22: 'the whole created universe groans in all its parts as if in the pangs of childbirth' (NEB). Verse 23: 'and not only the creation, but we ourselves . . groan inwardly.' What is this inward groaning

which we share with the rest of creation? What are the present sufferings of the church to which the apostle is referring? It is not now persecution, but the simple fact that we are only half saved!

It is a fact that not one of us is wholly saved yet. Our souls are redeemed, it is true, but not our bodies. And it is our unredeemed bodies which cause us to groan. Why is this? For one thing, these bodies are weak, fragile and mortal, subject to fatigue, sickness, pain and death. It is this that the apostle has in mind in 2 Corinthians 5 : 2, 4, when he says that in this body 'we groan'. But it is also that 'the flesh', our fallen sinful nature, dwells in our mortal bodies, 'sin which dwells within me' (7 : 17, 20). Indeed, it is this very indwelling sin which causes us to cry out, 'Wretched man that I am! Who will deliver me from this body of death?' Such a shout of anguish is precisely what Paul means by our present inward groaning, except that there the inward groan is audibly expressed.

What makes us groan inwardly, then, is our physical frailty on the one hand, and our fallen nature on the other. So we long ardently for the future glory, when we shall be delivered from both these burdens.

Our future glory is defined in two ways. First, it is 'the redemption of our bodies'. because we are going to be given new bodies on the last day, set free from their double burden, their frailty and their 'flesh'. Our resurrection bodies will have new, undreamed-of powers, and no indwelling sin.

The future glory is also called our 'adoption as sons'. The Greek word is the same as 'sonship' in verse 15. In one sense we have already received our adoption; in another sense we are still awaiting it, because our present sonship, although glorious, is imperfect. We are not yet conformed, either in body or in character, to the image of God's Son (see verse 29). Nor has our sonship yet been publicly revealed and recognized. But the last day will witness what in verse 19 is called 'the revealing of the sons of God'. The world does not yet know us as the children of God (1 Jn. 3 : 1), but on the last day it will be manifest. For then we shall obtain what is called 'the glorious liberty of the children of God' (verse 21). And the creation is going to obtain it with us.

Of this future, glorious inheritance we are absolutely sure. Why? Because (verse 23) we already 'have the first fruits of the Spirit'. We have not yet received our final 'adoption as sons'. We have not yet received 'the redemption of our bodies'. But we *have* received the Holy Spirit, the God-given guarantee of our full inheritance to come. Indeed, He is more than the guarantee of it; He is the foretaste of it. Sometimes Paul uses a commercial metaphor, and calls the Holy Spirit the 'earnest', the first instalment in a hire purchase agreement, the down payment which certifies that the remainder is going to be paid later. Here, however, the metaphor is agricultural, the first-fruits of the harvest being a pledge of the full crop to come.

So the Holy Spirit, who is the Spirit of sonship and makes us the children of God (verse 15), and then witnesses with our spirit that we are God's children (verse 16), is also Himself the pledge of our complete adoption to be the sons of God, when our bodies are redeemed.

Verses 24 and 25 enforce this further, asserting that 'in this hope we were saved'. We were saved, but only half saved, in hope of a full salvation in the end (to include our bodies). The object of that hope is invisible. We do not yet see it. But we wait for it with patient fortitude (*hupomonē*), undeterred by the grievous sufferings of this present time.

d. The Spirit helps our weakness in prayer (verses 26, 27)

Here is yet another ministry which the Holy Spirit fulfils. He is mentioned four times in the brief compass of these two verses. He 'helps us in our weakness', and the particular weakness here in view is our ignorance in prayer. 'We do not know how to pray as we ought', but the Spirit 'helps us in our weakness'.

The general ministry of the Holy Spirit in prayer is much neglected. Yet we are clearly told in Scripture that our access to the Father is not only through the Son, but by the Spirit (Eph. 2 : 18). The Holy Spirit's inspiration is as necessary as the Son's mediation if we are to gain access to the Father in prayer. But here the Holy Spirit's ministry in our prayer life is more specific.

It seems to be this. Sometimes, when believers do not know how to pray in words, they groan without words. Sometimes, to quote E. F. Kevan, 'we find ourselves brought to silence by the very intensity of our longings'. Or again, sometimes we feel so burdened by our mortality or by indwelling sin that we can only groan (as in the previous paragraph) 'with sighs too deep for words'. These unutterable sighs or groans (what J. B. Phillips calls 'those agonising longings which never find words') are not to be despised, as if we ought to put them into language. On the contrary, when we thus sigh with inarticulate desires, it is the Holy Spirit Himself interceding on our behalf, prompting these groans. We should not be ashamed of such wordless prayers. God the Father understands prayers which are sighed rather than said, because He searches our hearts, and can read our thoughts. He knows too what is the mind of the Spirit. because the Holy Spirit always prays according to the will of God.

And so the Father in heaven answers the prayers which are prompted by the Spirit in our hearts.

> *Prayer is the soul's sincere desire,*
>   *Uttered or unexpressed,*
> *The motion of a hidden fire*
>   *That trembles in the breast.*
>
> *Prayer is the burden of a sigh,*
>   *The falling of a tear,*
> *The upward glancing of an eye*
>   *When none but God is near.*

JAMES MONTGOMERY

These, then, are the four gracious activities of the Holy Spirit. He subdues our flesh, He witnesses to our sonship, He guarantees our inheritance, and He helps our weakness in prayer.

II. THE INVINCIBLE PURPOSE OF GOD
(8:28-39)

We know that in everything God works for good with those who love him, who are called according to his purpose. For those whom he foreknew he also pre-destined to be conformed to the image of his Son, in order that he might be the first-born among many brethren. And those whom he predestined he also called; and those whom he called he also justified; and those whom he justified he also glorified.

What then shall we say to this? If God is for us, who is against us? He who did not spare his own Son but gave him up for us all, will he not also give us all things with him? Who shall bring any charge against God's elect? It is God who justifies; who is to con-demn? Is it Christ Jesus, who died, yes, who was raised from the dead, who is at the right hand of God, who indeed intercedes for us? Who shall separate us from the love of Christ? Shall tribulation, or distress, or persecution, or famine, or nakedness, or peril, or sword? As it is written,

> *'For thy sake we are being killed all the day long; we are regarded as sheep to be slaughtered.'*

No, in all these things we are more than conquerors through him who loved us. For I am sure that neither death, nor life, nor angels, nor principalities, nor things present, nor things to come, nor powers, nor height, nor depth, nor anything else in all creation, will be able to separate us from the love of God in Christ Jesus our Lord.

This brings us to the conclusion, and the climax. In the last twelve verses of the chapter (28–39) the apostle rises to sublime heights unequalled anywhere in the New Testament. He does not now mention the Holy Spirit. Instead, having previously described some of the privileges of the justified—peace with God, union with Christ, freedom from the law, life in the Spirit—his great Spirit-directed mind now sweeps over the whole counsel of God, from an eternity that is past to an eternity that is yet to come, from the divine foreknowledge and predestination to the divine love from which absolutely nothing whatsoever is able to separate us.

The burden of the apostle's climax is the unchangeable, irresistible, invincible purpose of God, and by this purpose and in it, the eternal security of the people of God. These tremendous truths, far too great for our puny minds to absorb, Paul expresses first in a series of five undeniable affirmations, and then in a series of five unanswerable questions, in which he challenges anybody to contradict the affirmations which he has just made.

a. Five undeniable affirmations (verses 28–30)

He introduces his affirmations with a verse familiar to all believers (28). On it we have often stayed our troubled hearts and minds: 'We know that in everything God works for good with those who love him.' The AV is probably better known, 'all things work together for good to them that love God'. But the RSV is to be preferred because all things do not work themselves into a pattern for good; it is God who works all things together for good, including the pains and the groans of the previous paragraphs, in the case of 'those who love him, who are called according to his purpose'. Then follow the affirmations (verses 29, 30), which explain both what is meant by the divine calling and the sense in which God works all things together for good. This working together for good, God's purpose in the salvation of sinners, is traced from its beginnings in His own mind to its culmination in the eternal glory. The five stages are foreknowledge, predestination, calling, justification and glorification.

1 and 2. *He foreknew*, and *He predestined*. The difference between foreknowledge and predestination is perhaps that God's electing choice formed in His mind before He willed it. His decision preceded His decree. This is not the place to delve into the mysteries of predestination. Some wise and true words of the commentator C. J. Vaughan are worth quoting, however: 'Everyone who is eventually saved can only ascribe his salvation from the first step to the last to God's favour and act. Human merit must be excluded: and this can only be by tracing back the work far beyond the obedience which evidences, or even the

faith which appropriates, salvation; even to an act of
spontaneous favour on the part of that God who fore-
sees and foreordains from eternity all His works.'
Notice also that the purpose of the divine predestination is not favouritism, but holiness, Christlikeness. It
is that we should 'be conformed to the image of his
Son, in order that he might be the first-born among
many brethren'. Just as at the beginning, by an act of
sovereign grace, God created man in His own image,
so, again in sovereign grace, God predestined men to
be conformed to the image of His Son.

3 and 4. *He called*, and *He justified*. The call of God
is the historical outworking of His eternal predestination. Those whom God thus calls respond in faith to
the call, and those who thus believe, God justifies,
accepting them in Christ as His own.

5. *He glorified*, bringing to resurrection and to
heaven those whom He had predestined, called, and
justified, giving them new bodies in a new world. The
process of sanctification is omitted, but, as Professor
F. F. Bruce points out, it is involved in glorification:
'Sanctification is glory begun; glory is sanctification
completed.' So certain is this final stage of glorification
that it is even expressed by an aorist tense, as if it were
past, like the other stages which *are* past. It is a so-
called 'prophetic past'.

Here, then, is the apostle's series of five undeniable
affirmations. It is like a chain with five unbreakable
links: 'Those whom he foreknew he also predestined.
. . . And those whom he predestined he also called;
and those whom he called he also justified; and those
whom he justified he also glorified.' God is pictured as
moving steadily on from stage to stage—from an
eternal foreknowledge and predestination, through a
historical call and justification, to a final glorification
of His people in heaven.

b. Five unanswerable questions (verses 31–39)

'What then shall we say to this?' This is the little formula (used already three times in the chapters we have been studying) which the apostle uses to introduce some conclusion. He implies, in effect, 'In the light of what I have just said, what are we now going to say?' In the light of the foregoing, of the five great affirmations of verses 29 and 30, how shall we conclude? And Paul's answer to this question is to ask five more questions, to which there is no answer! Verse 31: 'If God is for us, who is against us?' Verse 32: 'He who did not spare his own Son but gave him up for us all, will he not also give us all things with him?' Verse 33: 'Who shall bring any charge against God's elect?' Verse 34: 'Who is to condemn?' Verse 35: 'Who shall separate us from the love of Christ?'

The apostle hurls these questions out into space, as it were, defiantly, triumphantly, challenging any creature in heaven or earth or hell to answer them or to deny the truth that is contained in them. But there is no answer, for nobody and nothing can harm the redeemed people of God. If we are to understand these unanswerable questions, it is important to see the reason why each remains unanswered. It is because the assertion implied in each is grounded upon some immovable truth. Thus each question, either explicitly or implicitly, is attached to an 'if' clause. This is clearest in the first one.

1. *'If God is for us, who is against us?'* (verse 31). Had Paul simply asked the question, 'Who is against us?', without the introductory clause, there would have been many replies. We have formidable enemies arrayed against us. Unbelievers are in opposition to us. Indwelling sin is a powerful force which assaults us. Death is an enemy. So is he who has the power of

death, the devil. In fact the world, the flesh and the devil are all too strong for us.

But Paul does not ask the simple question, 'Who is against us?' His question is: 'If God is for us'—the God who foreknew, predestined, called, justified and even glorified us, if *that* God is for us—'who is against us?' To that question there is no answer. The world, the flesh and the devil may still set themselves in array against us. But they can never prevail against us if God is on our side.

2. *'He who did not spare his own Son but gave him up for us all, will he not also give us all things with him?'* (verse 32). Again, if the apostle had merely asked, 'Will God not give us all things?' we might well have hummed and hawed, and given an equivocal answer. We need so many things, great and difficult things; how could we be certain that God will supply all our needs? But the way Paul expresses his question banishes our lingering doubts. The God whom we ask if He will give us all things is the God who has already given us His own Son. NEB translates: 'with this gift how can he fail to lavish upon us all he has to give?' If He gave His unspeakable, indescribable gift (His only Son, for sinners), will He not give us all lesser gifts which can easily be described? The cross proves the generosity of God.

3. *'Who shall bring any charge against God's elect?'* (verse 33). Commentators point out that the next two questions (about accusing and condemning us) seem to bring us, as it were, into a court of law. The argument is that no prosecution can be of any avail if Jesus Christ is our Advocate who pleads our cause, and if God the Judge has already justified us. Who will accuse us? Now again, if this question stood alone, it would not be at all difficult to answer. Our conscience accuses us. The devil never ceases to bring charges

against us, the devil who is called 'the accuser of the brethren', and whose very name means 'slanderer' or 'calumniator'. But the devil's accusations fall to the ground; they do not hurt us; they glance off us like arrows off a shield. Why? Because we are 'God's elect' whom He has justified, and if God has Himself justi-fied us, no accusation against us can stand.

4. *'Who is to condemn?'* (verse 34). Once again, many seek to. Sometimes our heart condemns us, or tries to (1 Jn. 3 : 20, 21). So do our critics and our enemies. Yes, and all the demons of hell. But their condemnations are idle nonsense. Why? Because of Christ Jesus. To begin with, He has died—died for the very sins for which otherwise we would indeed be con-demned. And Christ has been raised from the dead, to prove the efficacy of His death. And now He sits exalted at the Father's right hand, and there He is our heavenly Advocate interceding for us. With such a Christ as our Saviour—crucified, raised, exalted, inter-ceding on our behalf—we can confidently say 'there is therefore now no condemnation for those who are in Christ Jesus' (verse 1). We can call out even to the demons in hell, 'Which of you is going to condemn me?' And there will be no answer.

5. *'Who shall separate us from the love of Christ?'* (verse 35). With this fifth and last question, Paul him-self does what we have been trying to do with his other four questions. He looks round for a possible answer. He brings forward all the adversities he can think of, which might be thought to separate us from Christ's love. We may have to endure 'tribulation', 'distress' and 'persecution'—that is, the pressures of an ungodly world. We may have to undergo 'famine' and 'naked-ness'—that is, the lack of adequate food and clothing, which, since Jesus promised them to the heavenly Father's children, might seem to be evidence that God

does not care. We may even have to experience 'peril' and 'sword'—that is, the danger of death and actual death, by the malice of men; martyrdom, the ultimate test of our faith. It is a real test, too, because (verse 36) the Scripture warns us in Psalm 44:22 that God's people are for His sake 'being killed all the day long'. That is, they are continuously being exposed to the risk of death, like sheep for the slaughter.

These are adversities indeed. They are real sufferings, painful and perilous, and hard to bear. But can they separate us from the love of Christ? No! Verse 37: far from separating us from Christ's love, 'in all these things'—in these very sufferings, in the experience and endurance of them—'we are more than conquerors'. These five words represent only one in the Greek: *hypernikōmen*, meaning that we are 'hyper-conquerors'. Moreover, we are super-conquerors 'through him who loved us'. Notice that little phrase. It seems to say this: Christ has proved His love by His sufferings; therefore *our* sufferings cannot separate us from His love.

So Paul reaches his climax (verses 38 and 39). He begins, 'I am sure . . .'. This is my fixed, unshakable conviction, he says, that neither the crisis of death, nor the calamities of life, nor superhuman agencies, good or bad ('angels, principalities, powers'), nor time (whether present or future), nor space (whether height or depth), 'nor anything else in all creation' will be able, however hard it may try, 'to separate us from the love of God in Christ Jesus our Lord'—the love of God historically displayed in the death of Christ; the love of God poured into our hearts by the Spirit of Christ.

In that conviction of the love of God, through all the pains and perplexities of human experience, may we too both live and die!

CONCLUSION

The underlying theme of these chapters is that the Christian life is a new life—complete 'newness of life', in fact (6:4). Christians are indeed *Men Made New*. And each chapter contributes another feature to the portrait.

To begin with, 'we have peace with God'. We were enemies, but we have been reconciled. We live in a state of grace, in the favour of God, under His smile. And we rejoice in our confident expectation of the final glory.

Next, we have been united with Christ in His death and resurrection. This is what our baptism signified. The benefits of His death and the power of His resurrection are now ours because we are His.

Then also, we are freed from the dreadful tyranny of the law. Our relationship to God does not depend on our slavish obedience to rules and regulations. In Christ we are now under grace. This is the liberty with which Christ has set us free.

At the same time, we have the Holy Spirit Himself dwelling within us. And although we are no longer under obligation to keep the law to win our salvation, yet, having been saved, the righteous requirements of the law are fulfilled in us by the inward power of the Spirit. The same Spirit, who sanctifies us, also witnesses deep inside us that we are God's children, and helps us in our prayers.

And finally, we know that nothing can hinder the outworking of God's eternal purpose for us, or separate us from His unfailing love in Christ. One of the greatest of all Christian privileges is this knowledge of our absolute security amid the vicissitudes of life.

For these vicissitudes are many. There are tribulations inflicted by a hostile, unbelieving world. There is 'the flesh', the fallen nature which remains in the regenerate, 'sin which dwells within me', which dogs our footsteps, causing us to bemoan our wretchedness and to cry out for deliverance. There are also the sufferings to which we are prone as a part of the whole creation 'groaning in travail together'. External persecution, inward moral corruption, bodily frailty—these are our abiding problems. For all our privilege as Christians, we do not escape these.

If our Christian privilege does not insure us against these trials, it does not exempt us from obligations either. On the contrary, 'we are debtors' (8 : 12). Having become united to Christ in His death and resurrection, we must live the new life to which we have risen. Having yielded ourselves to God as His slaves, we must obey Him. Having received the Spirit, we must walk according to the Spirit. Having been given life, we must put to death all that is inconsistent with it.

Indeed, the more clearly we grasp the greatness of our Christian privilege, as *Men Made New*, the greater will be our Christian obligation to live accordingly, 'in newness of life', and the keener will be our longing to do so.